SLA

Other books in the
Opposing Viewpoints in World History series:

SLAVERY

James D. Torr, *Book Editor*

Daniel Leone, *President*
Bonnie Szumski, *Publisher*
Scott Barbour, *Managing Editor*
Helen Cothran, *Senior Editor*

OPPOSING VIEWPOINTS® SERIES

GREENHAVEN PRESS®

THOMSON
GALE

San Diego • Detroit • New York • San Francisco • Cleveland
New Haven, Conn. • Waterville, Maine • London • Munich

THOMSON

GALE

LIBRARY OF CONGRESS CATALOGING-IN-PUBLICATION DATA

Slavery : opposing viewpoints in world history / James D. Torr, book editor.
    p. cm. — (Opposing viewpoints in world history series)
    Includes bibliographical references and index.
    ISBN 0-7377-1706-8 (pbk. : alk. paper) — ISBN 0-7377-1705-X (lib. : alk. paper)
        1. Slavery—United States—History—Sources. 2. Antislavery movements—United States—History—Sources. I. Torr, James D., 1974– . II. Series.
    E441.S6365 2004
    306.3'62'0973—dc21   2003044812

 # Contents

Chapter 4: Slavery Divides a Nation

 **Foreword**

On December 2, 1859, several hundred soldiers gathered at the outskirts of Charles Town, Virginia, to carry out, and provide security for, the execution of a shabbily dressed old man with a beard that hung to his chest. The execution of John Brown quickly became and has remained one of those pivotal historical events that are immersed in controversy. Some of Brown's contemporaries claimed that he was a religious fanatic who deserved to be executed for murder. Others claimed Brown was a heroic and selfless martyr whose execution was a tragedy. Historians have continued to debate which picture of Brown is closest to the truth.

The wildly diverging opinions on Brown arise from fundamental disputes involving slavery and race. In 1859 the United States was becoming increasingly polarized over the issue of slavery. Brown believed in both the necessity of violence to end slavery and in the full political and social equality of the races. This made him part of the radical fringe even in the North. Brown's conviction and execution stemmed from his role in leading twenty-one white and black followers to attack and occupy a federal weapons arsenal in Harpers Ferry, Virginia. Brown had hoped to ignite a large slave uprising. However, the raid begun on October 16, 1859, failed to draw support from local slaves; after less than thirty-six hours, Brown's forces were overrun by federal and local troops. Brown was wounded and captured, and ten of his followers were killed.

Brown's raid—and its intent to arm slaves and foment insurrection—was shocking to the South and much of the North. An editorial in the *Patriot*, an Albany, Georgia, newspaper, stated that Brown was a "notorious old thief and murderer" who deserved to be hanged. Many southerners expressed fears that Brown's actions were part of a broader northern conspiracy against the South—fears that seemed to be confirmed by captured letters documenting Brown's ties with some prominent northern abolitionists, some of whom had provided him with financial support. Such alarms also found confirmation in the pronouncements of some speakers such as writer Henry David Thoreau, who asserted that

Brown had "a perfect right to interfere by force with the slave-holder, in order to rescue the slave." But not all in the North defended Brown's actions. Abraham Lincoln and William Seward, leading politicians of the nascent Republican Party, both denounced Brown's raid. Abolitionists, including William Lloyd Garrison, called Brown's adventure "misguided, wild, and apparently insane." They were afraid Brown had done serious damage to the abolitionist cause.

Today, though all agree that Brown's ideas on racial equality are no longer radical, historical opinion remains divided on just what Brown thought he could accomplish with his raid, or even whether he was fully sane. Historian Russell Banks argues that even today opinions of Brown tend to split along racial lines. African Americans tend to view him as a hero, Banks argues, while whites are more likely to judge him mad. "And it's for the same reason—because he was a white man who was willing to sacrifice his life to liberate Black Americans. The very thing that makes him seem mad to white Americans is what makes him seem heroic to Black Americans."

The controversy over John Brown's life and death remind readers that history is replete with debate and controversy. Not only have major historical developments frequently been marked by fierce debates as they happened, but historians examining the same events in retrospect have often come to opposite conclusions about their causes, effects, and significance. By featuring both contemporaneous and retrospective disputes over historical events in a pro/con format, the Opposing Viewpoints in World History series can help readers gain a deeper understanding of important historical issues, see how historical judgments unfold, and develop critical thinking skills. Each article is preceded by a concise summary of its main ideas and information about the author. An in-depth book introduction and prefaces to each chapter provide background and context. An annotated table of contents and index help readers quickly locate material of interest. Each book also features an extensive bibliography for further research, questions designed to spark discussion and promote close reading and critical thinking, and a chronology of events.

 Introduction

In the United States slavery is understandably associated with the South since it was the Southern states that so vigorously defended the practice during the nineteenth century. However, to understand how slavery first took hold in the South, historians look much farther back in time, to ancient Greece and Rome and the civilizations that preceded them. In many of these societies, it was common practice to enslave peoples who had been defeated in war. Even through the Middle Ages, Moors and Christians enslaved each other and justified it on religious grounds. Difficult as it is for us to understand today, slavery was a simple fact of life throughout much of human history.

During the fifteenth and sixteenth centuries, this unquestioning acceptance of slavery combined with two other factors—Europeans' belief in the inferiority of other races and cultures, and European settlement of the New World—to give rise to the Atlantic slave trade. According to historian James L. Stokesbury,

> When Europeans first made their way down the coast of Africa towards the east, and discovered the New World to the west, they still believed in slavery as an institution. Some men were free, some were slaves; God had made it that way. When the Spanish therefore enslaved the Indians, it was not to them a reprehensible act; the Church put limitations on what could be done, and attempted to prevent abuses in a social situation that was not itself regarded as an abuse. The first Negro slaves were actually imported for humanitarian reasons. Bishop Las Casas in the West Indies realized that the Indians made poor slaves and soon died off, so he recommended they be replaced by Negroes, who seemed more adaptable. His suggestion was taken up with such alacrity that he was soon appalled by it. . . . Within the first generation of settlement of the New World, the slave trade was a going thing, and there was no stopping it.

In the early seventeenth century, the British colonists in North America joined the Spanish in importing African slaves to the

New World. The slave trade eventually became more profitable in the New World than in Europe, in part because Europe already had a large supply of indigenous white labor. Historian David Brion Davis notes that "in the 320 years from 1500 to 1820, every European immigrant who arrived in the New World was matched by at least two African slaves." Economic realities further made slavery more important to the southern colonies of North America since they grew crops that required more hand cultivation and cheap labor.

Slavery Entrenched

At the time of the American Revolution, the split between North and South over the issue of slavery was apparent but not great enough to prevent the states from uniting as one nation. Delegates to the Constitutional Convention in 1787 forged a compromise on the issue of slavery: Among other constitutional provisions, a slave was to be counted as three-fifths of a person for purposes of taxation and representation. The Constitution's ambiguous position on slavery became a topic of considerable controversy during the nineteenth century, and modern historians still hold different views on the compromise the founding fathers forged. In 1975 historian John Hope Franklin charged that,

> having created a tragically flawed revolutionary doctrine and a Constitution that did *not* bestow the blessings of liberty on its posterity, the Founding Fathers set the stage for every succeeding generation to apologize, compromise, and temporize on the principles of liberty that were supposed to be the very foundation of our system of government and way of life.

Other historians contend that it would have been politically impossible for the framers of the Constitution both to make an unequivocal stand against slavery and unite the states into one nation, and so they chose the latter option. As University of Chicago professor Herbert J. Storing writes,

> The Founders did acknowledge slavery; they compromised with it. The effect was in the short run probably to strengthen it. . . . [But] in their accommodation to slavery, the Founders limited and confined it, and carefully withheld any indication

of moral approval, while they built a Union that they thought was the greatest instrument of human liberty ever made, that they thought would and indeed did lead to the extinction of Negro slavery.

Whatever the founding fathers' intentions, the compromise they forged staved off a national debate for only a few more decades. Meanwhile, economic realities continued to shape the slavery debate. With the beginning of the American industrial revolution in 1790, the Northern states' economies became more rooted in industry and commerce, making them less dependent on slave labor. By 1804 all of the Northern states had implemented plans to abolish slavery. But in the South the invention of laborsaving devices such as the water frame and the cotton gin made the plantation system more profitable and increased the demand for slaves.

There was a flurry of controversy in 1819, when Missouri applied for admission to the Union as a slave state. But the problem was solved with the Missouri Compromise, through which Missouri was admitted as a slave state while Maine was admitted as a

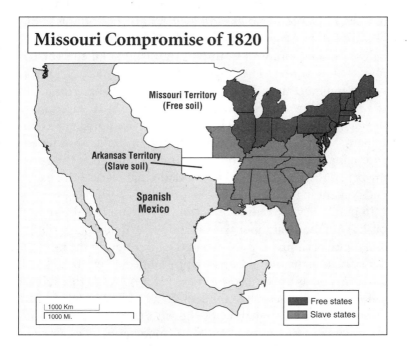

Missouri Compromise of 1820

Missouri Territory (Free soil)

Arkansas Territory (Slave soil)

Spanish Mexico

1000 Km
1000 Mi.

Free states
Slave states

free state. The issue of slavery was still largely a political rather than a moral one. According to slavery historian James Brewer Stewart, "Few Americans in the 1820s openly objected to slavery." But, he explains,

> on a much deeper level, a complex set of forces was at work during the 1820s which soon led, among white New Englanders, to an abolitionist movement of unparalleled scope and intensity. Inspired by Christian egalitarianism and a profound sense of personal guilt, young men and women were soon to take up the immense task of convincing their countrymen that slavery was a terrible sin, and that race prejudice was at war with the teachings of Jesus.

While antislavery societies had existed before the 1820s, during this decade the abolitionist movement began to take on a more vocal, fervent, and confrontational character.

Slavery Condemned

Many historians recognize 1831 as the year that the national debate over slavery entered its most contentious phase. It was in this year that lay preacher and former slave Nat Turner led a slave rebellion in Southampton County, Virginia, that killed approximately sixty whites. The Southampton revolt was quickly put down, and more than one hundred blacks were hanged for it, but the rebellion profoundly affected the South. It raised fears throughout the South that a larger general slave uprising was imminent. Many Southerners blamed Northern abolitionists for encouraging slave rebellion, but abolitionists noted that the uprising belied slaveholders' traditional claim that blacks were happy and content in bondage.

In the same year, radical abolitionist William Lloyd Garrison broke with moderate abolitionists and began denouncing slavery as a national sin in his publication the *Liberator*. In the newspaper's opening manifesto Garrison proclaimed, "I *will* be as harsh as truth, and as uncompromising as justice. . . . On this subject [abolition] I do not wish to think or speak, or write, with moderation. No! No! Tell a man whose house is on fire to give a moderate alarm . . . but urge me not to use moderation in a cause like the present." According to Garrison biographer Henry Mayer,

> No editor has ever produced a newspaper of agitation for longer than Garrison sustained *The Liberator*, which appeared weekly without interruption for thirty-five years and did not cease publication until the ratification of the Thirteenth Amendment. . . . With ferocious determination, Garrison broke the silence and made the public listen in a way his predecessors had not. . . . He made the moral issue of slavery so palpable it could not be evaded.

Initially, Garrison's fellow Bostonians disliked his provocative stance almost as much as Southerners did. In October 1835 Garrison narrowly escaped a proslavery mob intent on lynching him. Slowly but surely, however, abolitionist sentiment grew. "By the 1850s," writes historian Robert Elliott MacDougall, "new mobs were forming in the city, this time to protest the capture of runaway slaves."

Southerners defended their "peculiar institution" just as vehemently as the radical abolitionists condemned it. Some, such as Virginia reverend Thornton Stringfellow, cited biblical passages to justify slavery in order to refute the religious arguments of the abolitionists. "In Genesis xvii," Stringfellow wrote, "we are informed of a covenant God entered into with Abraham. . . . He expressly stipulates, that Abraham shall put the token of this covenant upon every servant born in his house, and upon every servant *bought with his money*." Furthermore, according to Stringfellow, "Jesus Christ has not abolished slavery by a prohibitory command."

Other defenders of slavery used more secular reasoning to argue that slavery was a positive social good. South Carolina statesman James Henry Hammond, in his famous 1858 "Mud-Sill" speech, claimed that white racial superiority justified slavery:

> In all social systems there must be a class to do the menial duties, to perform the drudgery of life. That is, a class requiring but a low order of intellect and but little skill. Its requisites are vigor, docility, fidelity. Such a class you must have, or you would not have that other class which leads progress, civilization, and refinement. It constitutes the very mud-sill

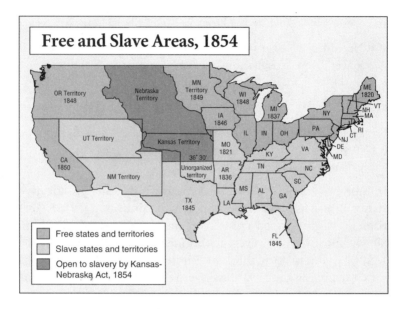

Free and Slave Areas, 1854

- Free states and territories
- Slave states and territories
- Open to slavery by Kansas-Nebraska Act, 1854

[foundation] of society and of political government; and you might as well attempt to build a house in the air, as to build either the one or the other, except on this mud-sill. Fortunately for the South, she found a race adapted to that purpose to her hand. A race inferior to her own, but eminently qualified in temper, in vigor, in docility, in capacity to stand the climate, to answer all her purposes. We use them for our purpose, and call them slaves.

In 1854 proslavery writer George Fitzhugh claimed that slaves were treated better in the South than were white workers in Northern factories: "There is no rivalry, no competition to get employment among slaves, as among free laborers. . . . The slaves are well fed, well clad, have plenty of fuel, and are happy."

Slavery Abolished

Throughout the 1830s, 1840s, and 1850s, abolitionists and slavery's defenders each refined and reiterated their arguments. North and South became increasingly alienated and, as the radical abolitionists had envisioned, less willing to compromise over the issue of slavery. Finally, when antislavery candidate Abraham Lincoln was elected in 1860, Southern secession and the Civil War followed. America's long debate over slavery was finally settled by violence and bloodshed.

The Thirteenth Amendment abolished slavery in 1865; each generation since then has had to grapple with the legacy of slavery, which includes racism, economic inequality between blacks and whites, and sectional tension between North and South. Moreover, America's history as a slaveholding nation continues to challenge the ideals that most Americans have about themselves and their nation. As David Brion Davis explains,

> It was African slaves and their descendants who furnished the basic labor power that created dynamic New World economies and the first international mass markets for such consumer goods as sugar, rice, tobacco, dyestuffs, and cotton. Yet, from the outset, the New World was seen by many, like the biblical Promised Land, as a space for new beginnings, for possibilities that would break free from the coercive bondage of the past. Paradoxically, the debasement of millions of workers . . . appeared to liberate other human beings to take control of their destiny. . . . This profound contradiction lay close to the core of the self-presentation of the new United States, which was "conceived in liberty" but based on slave labor, dedicated to certain "propositions" or principles, such as "all men are created equal," but no less committed to compromises that protected the autonomy and political power of men who owned human property.

The failure of the founding fathers to recognize slavery as antithetical to their ideals; the economics of Southern agriculture; the threat of slave rebellion; the zeal of abolitionists; the determination of slaveholders to defend their way of life; the compromises between North and South; and ultimately the reality of secession and war—the issue of slavery encompasses all of these topics and more. The selections in *Opposing Viewpoints in World History: Slavery* explore these issues, offering a variety of perspectives from slaves, slaveholders, abolitionists, and modern scholars.

CHAPTER 1

Moral Issues Surrounding Slavery

 # Chapter Preface

When the founding fathers assembled at the Constitutional Convention in 1787, slavery was firmly established in the five southernmost states. But as Stanford University historian Don E. Fehrenbacher notes,

> Slavery was an institution under severe scrutiny, both as a matter of conscience and as a matter of public interest. Many Americans were finding it difficult to square slaveholding with the principles of Christianity, and many were troubled by the contrast between the celebration of human freedom in the Declaration of Independence and the presence of human servitude throughout so much of the Republic.

Despite these concerns, in the nation's first decades slavery was only abolished where it was unprofitable. And as Harvard historian Nathan Irving Huggins writes, "The Founding Fathers . . . did not address frankly and openly, in any of their official documents, the conspicuous fact of racial slavery." The U.S. Constitution, for example, does not mention the words *slave* or *slavery* at all. Proslavery sentiment was rooted deep in racism and in Southern social and economic interests, and antislavery sentiment was simply not, in Fehrenbacher's words, "intense enough to become a prime motive force."

It took eighty more years for slavery to become the focus of American politics, and when it did, it plunged the nation into a bloody civil war. Though it cost over six hundred thousand lives, the Civil War seemed to settle the issue of slavery. The Thirteenth Amendment made slavery illegal, and, over time, Americans reached a consensus that slavery was morally wrong.

But difficult moral issues surrounding slavery remain with us today. Just as Americans of the eighteenth and nineteenth centuries had trouble reconciling the phrase "all men are created equal" with the existence of slavery, modern students of history are challenged to reconcile America's emphasis on individual freedom and equality with its history of slavery and racism.

Americans' discomfort with the historical reality of slavery was made evident in 1997, when DNA tests showed a strong likelihood that Thomas Jefferson had an ongoing sexual relationship with one of his slaves, Sally Hemmings. The story led many Americans to grapple with one of America's greatest historical ironies: The man who wrote the Declaration of Independence owned more than two hundred slaves. Americans' different reactions to the Jefferson-Hemmings story revealed their different views of slavery and of America itself. The debate over whether being a slaveholder tainted Jefferson's character paralleled a larger debate over how being a slaveholding nation had tainted U.S. society. As *Washington Post* reporter Ken Ringle put it, "Those who see the nation as a caldron of racism and hypocrisy can take the story as proof of white denial of the abusive racial sins of our forefathers. Those who see the United States as the wellspring of liberty can view the relationship as one of human desire dwarfed by Jefferson's soaring vision of the rights of man."

America's long national debate over the morality of slavery ended with the Civil War, but the moral legacy of slavery remains. The viewpoints in the following chapter explore both antebellum views of slavery and historical controversies about slavery and its aftermath.

Viewpoint 1

"Where two races of different origin . . . are brought together, the relation now existing in the slaveholding States between the two, is, instead of an evil, a good—a positive good."

Slavery Is a Positive Good

John C. Calhoun

From 1811 until his death in 1850 South Carolina statesman John C. Calhoun served successfully as a congressman, secretary of war, vice president, senator, secretary of state, and again as a senator. In the 1830s, as the abolitionist movement gained momentum in the North, Calhoun developed an influential political and ideological defense of slavery. The following viewpoint is excerpted from a speech Calhoun gave before the Senate on February 6, 1837, in which he addresses a series of petitions to abolish slavery that Congress had received. Calhoun proclaims slavery to be a "positive good." Echoing the Greek philosopher Aristotle, Calhoun argues that in all societies one class lives partly off the labor of another, and that Southern masters care for their laborers better than employers in the North or in Europe do. He also warns that the zeal of the abolitionist movement in the North threatens to divide the United States.

John C. Calhoun, address to the U.S. Senate, February 6, 1837.

We of the South will not, cannot surrender our institutions. To maintain the existing relations between the two races, inhabiting that section of the Union, is indispensable to the peace and happiness of both. It cannot be subverted without drenching the country in blood, and extirpating one or the other of the races. Be it good or bad, it has grown up with our society and institutions, and is so interwoven with them, that to destroy it would be to destroy us as a people. But let me not be understood as admitting, even by implication, that the existing relations between the two races in the slaveholding States is an evil:—far otherwise; I hold it to be a good, as it has thus far proved itself to be to both, and will continue to prove so if not disturbed by the fell spirit of abolition.

A Benefit to Blacks

I appeal to facts. Never before has the black race of Central Africa, from the dawn of history to the present day, attained a condition so civilized and so improved, not only physically, but morally and intellectually. It came among us in a low, degraded, and savage condition, and in the course of a few generations it has grown up under the fostering care of our institutions, reviled as they have been, to its present comparatively civilized condition. This, with the rapid increase of numbers, is conclusive proof of the general happiness of the race, in spite of all the exaggerated tales to the contrary.

In the mean time, the white or European race has not degenerated. It has kept pace with its brethren in other sections of the Union where slavery does not exist. It is odious to make comparison; but I appeal to all sides whether the South is not equal in virtue, intelligence, patriotism, courage, disinterestedness, and all the high qualities which adorn our nature. I ask whether we have not contributed our full share of talents and political wisdom in forming and sustaining this political fabric; and whether we have not constantly inclined most strongly to the side of liberty, and been the first to see and first to resist the encroachments of power. In one thing only are we inferior—the arts of gain; we acknowledge that we are less wealthy than the Northern section of this Union, but I trace this mainly to the fiscal action of this Government, which has extracted much from, and spent little among us. Had it been the reverse,—if the exaction had been from the other section, and the expenditure with us, this point of superiority would not be against us now, as it was not

Happy and Contented Slaves

John C. Calhoun's defense of slavery as a "positive good" was extremely influential in the South. In a famous March 4, 1858, speech, South Carolina senator James Henry Hammond elaborated on Calhoun's argument, emphasizing how slavery benefited slaveholders and slaves alike.

In all social systems there must be a class to do the menial duties, to perform the drudgery of life. That is, a class requiring but a low order of intellect and but little skill. Its requisites are vigor, docility, fidelity. Such a class you must have, or you would not have that other class which leads progress, civilization, and refinement. It constitutes the very mud-sill [foundation] of society and of political government; and you might as well attempt to build a house in the air, as to build either the one or the other, except on this mud-sill. Fortunately for the South, she found a race adapted to that purpose to her hand. A race inferior to her own, but eminently qualified in temper, in vigor, in docility, in capacity to stand the climate, to answer all her purposes. We use them for our purpose, and call them slaves.

Our slaves are black, of another and inferior race. The *status* in which we have placed them is an elevation. They are elevated from the condition in which God first created them, by being made our slaves. None of that race on the whole face of the globe can be compared with the slaves of the South. They are happy, content, unaspiring, and utterly incapable, from intellectual weakness, ever to give us any trouble by their aspirations.

James Henry Hammond, "Speech on the Admission of Kansas," U.S. Senate, March 4, 1858.

at the formation of this Government.

But I take higher ground. I hold that in the present state of civilization, where two races of different origin, and distinguished by color, and other physical differences, as well as intellectual, are brought together, the relation now existing in the slaveholding States between the two, is, instead of an evil, a good—a positive good. I feel myself called upon to speak freely upon the subject where the honor and interests of those I represent are involved. I hold then, that there never has yet existed a wealthy and civilized society in which one portion of the community did not, in point of fact, live on the labor of the other. Broad and general as is this assertion, it is fully borne out by history. This is not the proper occasion, but if it were, it would not be difficult to trace the various devices by which the wealth of all civilized communities has been so unequally divided, and to show by what means so small a share has been allotted to those by whose labor it was produced, and so large a share given to the non-producing classes. The devices are almost innumerable, from the brute force and gross superstition of ancient times, to the subtle and artful fiscal contrivances of modern. I might well challenge a comparison between them and the more direct, simple, and patriarchal mode by which the labor of the African race is, among us, commanded by the European. I may say with truth, that in few countries so much is left to the share of the laborer, and so little exacted from him, or where there is more kind attention paid to him in sickness or infirmities of age. Compare his condition with the tenants of the poor houses in the more civilized portions of Europe—look at the sick, and the old and infirm slave, on one hand, in the midst of his family and friends, under the kind superintending care of his master and mistress, and compare it with the forlorn and wretched condition of the pauper in the poor house.

A Stable Economic and Social System

But I will not dwell on this aspect of the question; I turn to the political; and here I fearlessly assert that the existing relation between the two races in the South, against which these blind fanatics are waging war, forms the most solid and durable foundation on which to rear free and stable political institutions. It is useless to disguise the fact. There is and always has been in an advanced stage of wealth and civilization, a conflict between labor and capital. The condition of society in the South exempts us from the disorders and dangers resulting from this conflict; and which explains why it is that the political condition of the slaveholding States has been so much more stable and quiet than that of the North. The advantages of the former, in this respect, will become more and more manifest if left undisturbed by interference from without, as the country advances in wealth and numbers.

We have, in fact, but just entered that condition of society where the strength and durability of our political institutions are to be tested; and I venture nothing in predicting that the experience of the next generation will fully test how vastly more favorable our condition of society is to that of other sections for free and stable institutions, provided we are not disturbed by the interference of others, or shall have sufficient intelligence and spirit to resist promptly and successfully such interference. It rests with ourselves to meet and repel them. I look not for aid to this Government, or to the other States; not but there are kind feelings towards us on the part of the great body of the non-slaveholding States; but as kind as their feelings may be, we may rest assured that no political party in those States will risk their ascendency for our safety. If we do not defend ourselves none will defend us; if we yield we will be more and more pressed as we recede; and if we submit we will be trampled under foot. Be assured that emancipation itself would not satisfy these fanatics:—that gained, the next step would· be to raise the negroes to a social and political equality with the whites; and that being effected, we would soon find the present condition of the two races reversed. They and their northern allies would be the masters, and we the slaves.

Viewpoint 2

"There is not a man on earth who does not believe that slavery is a curse."

Slavery Is Evil

Theodore Dwight Weld

Theodore Dwight Weld rivals fellow abolitionist William Lloyd Garrison as the leading figure in the American antislavery movement. Weld helped found the American Anti-Slavery Society, directing its New York Office and serving as editor of the society's newspaper the *Emancipator* from 1836 to 1840. He also directed the national campaign for sending antislavery petitions to Congress.

Though not published under his own name, Weld's most famous book is *American Slavery as It Is*, a book that Weld wrote and edited with his wife, Angelina Grimké, and sister-in-law, Sarah Grimké. Published in 1839, *American Slavery as It Is* sold thousands of copies, and Harriet Beecher Stowe partly based her antislavery novel *Uncle Tom's Cabin* on it. It is considered one of the most influential publications of the antislavery movement. The book is primarily a compilation of articles and notices from Southern newspapers documenting the cruelties of slavery. The excerpt below includes Weld's introduction to the documents. He attacks the morality of slavery and the character of slaveholders. None of Weld's speeches have been recorded, but this viewpoint gives an idea of his effectiveness as a speaker against slavery.

Theodore Dwight Weld, *American Slavery as It Is; Testimony of a Thousand Witnesses*. New York: American Anti-Slavery Society, 1839.

Reader, you are impaneled as a juror to try a plain case and bring in an honest verdict. The question at issue is not one of law but of fact—What is the actual condition of the slaves in the United States? A plainer case never went to a jury. Look at it. TWENTY-SEVEN HUNDRED THOUSAND PERSONS in this country, men, women, and children, are in SLAVERY. Is slavery, as a condition for human beings, good, bad, or indifferent? We submit the question without argument. You have common sense, and conscience, and a human heart—pronounce upon it. You have a wife, or a husband, a child, a father, a mother, a brother, or a sister—make the case your own, make it theirs, and bring in your verdict.

The Verdict Is Guilty

The case of Human Rights against Slavery has been adjudicated in the court of conscience times innumerable. The same verdict has always been rendered—"Guilty"; the same sentence has always been pronounced, "Let it be accursed"; and human nature, with her million echoes, has rung it round the world in every language under heaven, "Let it be accursed. Let it be accursed." His heart is false to human nature who will not say "Amen." There is not a man on earth who does not believe that slavery is a curse. Human beings may be inconsistent, but human *nature* is true to herself. She has uttered her testimony against slavery with a shriek ever since the monster was begotten; and till it perishes amidst the execrations of the universe, she will traverse the world on its track, dealing her bolts upon its head, and dashing against it her condemning brand.

We repeat it, every man knows that slavery is a curse. Whoever denies this, his lips libel his heart. Try him; clank the chains in his ears and tell him they are for *him*. Give him an hour to prepare his wife and children for a life of slavery. Bid him make haste and get ready their necks for the yoke, and their wrists for the coffle chains, then look at his pale lips and trembling knees, and you have *nature's* testimony against slavery.

Two million seven hundred thousand persons in these states are in this condition. They were made slaves and are held such by force, and by being put in fear, and this for no crime! Reader, what have you to say of such treatment? Is it right, just, benevolent? Suppose I should seize you, rob you of your liberty, drive you into the field, and make you work without pay as long as you live—would that be justice and kindness, or monstrous injustice and cruelty?

Now, everybody knows that the slaveholders do these things to the slaves every day, and yet it is stoutly affirmed that they treat them well and kindly, and that their tender regard for their slaves restrains the masters from inflicting cruelties upon them. We shall go into no metaphysics to show the absurdity of this pretense. The man who *robs* you every day is, forsooth, quite too tenderhearted ever to cuff or kick you!

Gentle Oppression

True, he can snatch your money, but he does it gently lest he should hurt you. He can empty your pockets without qualms, but if your *stomach* is empty, it cuts him to the quick. He can make you work a lifetime without pay, but loves you too well to let you go hungry. He fleeces you of your *rights* with a relish, but is shocked if you work bareheaded in summer or in winter without warm stockings. He can make you go without your *liberty*, but never without a shirt. He can crush, in you, all hope of bettering your condition by vowing that you shall die his slave, but, though he can coolly torture your feelings, he is too compassionate to lacerate your back; he can break your heart, but he is very tender of your skin. He can strip you of all protection and thus expose you to all outrages, but if you are exposed to the *weather*, half-clad and half-sheltered, how yearn his tender bowels!

What! Slaveholders talk of treating men well, and yet not only rob them of all they get, and as fast as they get it, but rob them of *themselves*, also; their very hands and feet, and all their muscles, and limbs, and senses, their bodies and minds, their time and liberty and earnings, their free speech and rights of conscience, their right to acquire knowledge and property and reputation; and yet they who plunder them of all these would fain make us believe that their soft hearts ooze out so lovingly toward their slaves that they always keep them well-housed and well-clad, never push them too hard in the field, never make their dear backs smart, nor let their dear stomachs get empty.

But there is no end to these absurdities. Are slaveholders dunces, or do they take all the rest of the world to be, that they think to bandage our eyes with such thin gauzes? Protesting their kind regard for those whom they hourly plunder of all they have and all they get! What! When they have seized their victims and annihilated all their *rights*, still claim to be the special guardians of their *happiness!* Plunderers of their liberty, yet the careful suppliers of their wants? Robbers of their earnings, yet watchful sentinels round their interests, and kind providers of their comforts? Filching all their time, yet granting generous donations for rest and sleep? Stealing the use of their muscles, yet thoughtful of their ease? Putting them under drivers, yet careful that they are not hard-pushed? Too humane, forsooth, to stint the stomachs of their slaves, yet force their *minds* to starve, and brandish over them pains and penalties if they dare to reach forth for the smallest crumb of knowledge, even a letter of the alphabet!

It is no marvel that slaveholders are always talking of their *kind treatment* of their slaves. The only marvel is that men of sense can be gulled by such professions. Despots always insist that they are merciful. The greatest tyrants that ever dripped with blood have assumed the titles of "most gracious," "most clement," "most merciful," etc., and have ordered their crouching vassals to accost them thus. When did not vice lay claim to those virtues which are the opposites of its habitual crimes? The guilty, according to their own showing, are always innocent, and cowards brave, and drunkards sober, and harlots chaste, and pickpockets honest to a fault. . . .

False Testimonies

As slaveholders and their apologists are volunteer witnesses in their own cause and are flooding the world with testimony that their slaves are kindly treated; that they are well-fed, well-clothed, well-housed, well-lodged, moderately worked, and bountifully provided with all things needful for their comfort, we propose, first, to disprove their assertions by the testimony of a multitude of impartial witnesses, and then to put slaveholders themselves through a course of cross-questioning which shall draw their condemnation out of their own mouths.

We will prove that the slaves in the United States are treated with barbarous inhumanity; that they are overworked, underfed, wretchedly clad and lodged, and have insufficient sleep; that they are often made to wear round their necks iron collars armed with prongs, to drag heavy chains and weights at their feet while working in the field, and to wear yokes, and bells, and iron horns; that they are often kept confined in the stocks day and night for weeks together, made to wear gags in their mouths for hours or days, have some of their front teeth torn out or broken off that they may be easily detected when they run away; that they are frequently flogged with terrible severity, have red pepper rubbed into their lacerated flesh, and hot brine, spirits of turpentine, etc., poured over the gashes to increase the torture; that they are often stripped naked, their backs and limbs cut with knives, bruised and mangled by scores and hundreds of blows with the paddle, and terribly torn by the claws of cats, drawn over them by their tormentors; that they are often hunted with bloodhounds and shot down like beasts, or torn in pieces by dogs; that they are often suspended by the arms and whipped and beaten till they faint, and, when revived by restoratives, beaten again till they faint, and sometimes till they die; that their ears are often cut off, their eyes knocked out, their bones broken, their flesh branded with red hot irons; that they are maimed, mutilated, and burned to death over slow fires. All these things, and more, and worse, we shall *prove*. Reader, we know whereof we affirm, we have weighed it well; *more and worse* WE WILL PROVE. . . .

The barbarous indifference with which slaveholders regard the forcible sundering of husbands and wives, parents and children, brothers and sisters, and the unfeeling brutality indicated by the language in which they describe the efforts made by the slaves, in their yearnings after those from whom they have been torn away, reveals a "public opinion" toward them as dead to their agony as if they were cattle. It is well-nigh impossible to open a Southern paper without finding evidence of this. Though the truth of this assertion can hardly be called in question, we subjoin a few illustrations, and could easily give hundreds. . . .

Runaway Advertisements

From the *Southern Argus*, Oct. 31, 1837.

"Runaway—my negro man, Frederick, about 20 years of age.

He is no doubt near the plantation of G.W. Corprew, Esq. of Noxubbee county, Mississippi, as *his wife belongs to that gentleman, and he followed her from my residence.* The above reward will be paid to any one who will confine him in jail and inform me of it at Athens, Ala.

"Athens, Alabama.

Kerkman Lewis."

From the *Savannah* (Ga.) *Republican,* May 24, 1838.

"$40 Reward.—Ran away from the subscriber in Savannah, his negro girl Patsey. She was purchased among the gang of negroes, known as the Hargreave's estate. She is no doubt lurking about Liberty county, at which place *she has relatives.*

Edward Houstoun, of Florida."

. . . From the *Norfolk* (Va.) *Beacon,* March 31, 1838.

"The subscriber will give $20 for the apprehension of his negro woman, Maria, who ran away about twelve months since. She is known to be lurking in or about Chuckatuch, in the county of Nansemond, where *she has a husband,* and *formerly belonged.*

Peter Oneill."

From the *Macon* (Ga.) *Messenger,* Jan. 16, 1839.

"Ranaway from the subscriber, two negroes, Davis, a man about 45 years old; also Peggy, his wife, near the same age. Said negroes will probably make their way to Columbia county, as *they have children* living in that county. I will liberally reward any person who may deliver them to me.

Nehemiah King."

. . . From the *Richmond* (Va.) *Enquirer,* Feb. 20, 1838.

"$10 Reward for a negro woman, named Sally, 40 years old. We have just reason to believe the said negro to be now lurking on the James River Canal, or in the Green Spring neighborhood, where, we are informed, *her husband resides.* The above reward will be given to any person *securing* her.

Polly C. Shields.
Mount Elba, Feb. 19, 1838."

"$50 Reward.—Ranaway from the subscriber, his negro man Pauladore, commonly called Paul. I understand Gen. R.Y. Hayne *has purchased his wife and children* from H.L. Pinckney, Esq. and has them now on his plantation at Goosecreek, where, no doubt, the fellow is frequently *lurking*.

T. Davis."

. . ."Stop the Runaway!!!—$25 Reward. Ranaway from the Eagle Tavern, a negro fellow, named Nat. He is no doubt attempting to *follow his wife, who was lately sold to a speculator* named Redmond. The above reward will be paid by Mrs. Lucy M. Downman, of Sussex county, Va."

Multitudes of advertisements like the above appear annually in the Southern papers. Reader, look at the preceding list—mark the unfeeling barbarity with which their masters and *mistresses* describe the struggles and perils of sundered husbands and wives, parents and children, in their weary midnight travels through forests and rivers, with torn limbs and breaking hearts, seeking the embraces of each other's love. In one instance, a mother, torn from all her children and taken to a remote part of another state, presses her way back through the wilderness, hundreds of miles, to clasp once more her children to her heart; but, when she has arrived within a few miles of them, in the same county, is discovered, seized, dragged to jail, and her purchaser told, through an advertisement, that she awaits his order. But we need not trace out the harrowing details already before the reader.

Viewpoint 3

"Most slaves lived in squalor, ate and dressed poorly, and died early deaths."

Slavery Was Oppressive and Dehumanizing

Robert Liston

In his book *Slavery in America*, author Robert Liston offers an overview of slave life in the Old South in the first half of the nineteenth century. He acknowledges that some slaves were treated relatively well by their masters, but also notes that some were treated with sadism and brutality. Between these extremes, he writes, the typical slave lived a life of constant toil. Whipping was the most common punishment for unproductive slaves. Most slaves lived in shacks and were chronically undernourished. Mortality rates and average lifespans were significantly worse for blacks in the Old South than for whites. Beyond these oppressive living conditions, concludes Liston, the worst part of slavery was that slaves were treated as property rather than as human beings.

By 1860, when the last census prior to the Civil War was taken, there were just under four million slaves in the United States.

Robert Liston, *Slavery in America: The History of Slavery*. New York: McGraw-Hill, 1970. Copyright © 1970 by McGraw-Hill. Reproduced by permission.

That figure reveals the truly fantastic growth of slavery in this country. There had been 700,000 in 1790. The million mark was reached in 1810. Twenty years later there were two million slaves, a figure which doubled again in the next three decades. The same census counted only 488,000 free Negroes in the United States, thus clearly showing how thoroughly the black race was subjugated in this country. . . .

To understand the institution of slavery as practiced in the United States, one must appreciate the magnitude of it. There were four million slaves spread over an area of more than 700,000 square miles, from Delaware to Florida, the Atlantic coast to Missouri, Arkansas, and Texas.

With so many slaves living on isolated farms and plantations over so vast an area, almost any statement made about slavery, slave conditions, slave attitudes, and treatment of slaves is true. For example, it is true, as the apologists for slavery loved to trumpet, that some slaves were treated kindly by their masters and enjoyed better housing, clothing, food, and working conditions than immigrant white workers in the North. It is also true that some slaves owners inflicted the most inhuman treatment on their slaves. A Georgia slave owner, Thomas Sorrell, was found guilty of killing one of his slaves with an axe, but the jury recommended that the court be lenient with him. There are numerous records of masters or mistresses beating slaves on the face as well as the body. A Mrs. Alpheus Lewis, according to records, burned her slave girl around the neck with hot tongs. A drunken Kentucky master dismembered his slave and threw him piece by piece into the fire. A Mississippi master inflicted over one thousand lashes on a slave whom he suspected of stealing.

The point of these examples is that neither the good treatment nor the barbaric treatment is typical. Most slave owners were neither so good nor so bad, but so widespread was the practice of slavery that examples of nearly every type can be found. . . .

Historians and other scholars have had a staggering task in trying to discover and report the nature of slavery in the United States. They have had to piece together, like a huge jigsaw puzzle, a picture of slavery. Many sources have been used—plantation records, diaries and autobiographies of slaveholders, letters, newspaper advertisements, accounts by travelers such as Frederick Law Olmsted, and remembrances of former slaves. The problem is to evaluate the importance of the information. Ex-slave Frederick Douglass gave a superb account of his slavery experiences, but were his typical? Or were slaves treated differently on the neighboring plantations? Another problem is that the slaveholders tended to present a biased view of themselves. It was only natural for them to portray their actions and motives in a highly favorable light. . . .

Slave Life

Despite its imperfections, a picture of slavery exists today. It isn't very pretty.

The statistically typical slave lived on a plantation of twenty or more bondmen. The practices of the plantation varied with its size and location, the crop it produced, and the disposition of the planter. But there was a general uniformity to plantation life. By 1860, when human slavery had been perfected in the South, there existed a well-defined set of rules for managing a plantation. Agricultural magazines of the South regularly carried articles on plantation management and slave management. The standard practices were usually those developed by large planters who had many slaves. After all, the big slave owners were the wealthiest, best educated, and most successful planters. It was only natural for smaller, less successful men to copy them. Fortunately for the historian, it is the wealthy planter who left the most copious records of his operations.

The purpose of a plantation was to make money. Like businessmen everywhere, the planter put his effort and talent into running his plantation so as to make the most money at the least cost. The plantation has been compared to a factory. Most often, it was a factory for producing cotton. As in a factory, the planter had his labor divided into specialties. Most were field hands—plowing, planting, hoeing, picking, ginning, and baling cotton. There were hands who specialized in each of those functions and who were expected to train the slave children as they grew up. Some slaves were trained in carpentry, smithery, mechanics, and in other specialties. Other slaves were trained to care for the slave babies, so that the mothers would be free to work in the fields. There were slave cooks, who prepared the food for the other slaves, so little time would be lost in eating. Slaves were used as seamstresses to make the rude clothing worn by the slaves. Then there were the domestic servants—butlers, maids, cooks, housekeepers, stablemen, and coachmen—who provided the creature comforts valued by the planters. Resident physicians took care of health needs, and there were accountants, business managers, foremen, and overseers.

Only the wealthiest planters had such a high degree of specialization, but all planters had some of it and wished for more.

Constant Toil

From the slave's point of view, the plantation system could be described in a single word: work. The day began with the ringing of a bell or the sounding of a horn half an hour before daylight. In the semidarkness, the slaves had a few minutes to get up, get dressed, gulp some breakfast, prepare the food they would eat at noon, and go to work in the fields. There was so little time that it was not uncommon for slaves to be seen dressing as they walked or ran to the fields.

At first daylight, or "day clean" as it was called, a second bell or horn sounded. The day's work had begun. It lasted, typically, until first dusk, after which the slaves had to do their chores, such as putting away tools, feeding livestock, tending gardens. Only then could they prepare their evening meals. Invariably they were exhausted from a day of backbreaking toil and fell asleep. . . .

The slave's life was a life of toil. Solomon Northrup, a free Negro who was kidnapped and held in bondage in Louisiana for twelve years, told his story to a Northerner who wrote Northrup's autobiography. It contains this passage:

> The hands are required to be in the cotton field as soon as it is light in the morning, and, with the exception of 10 or 15 minutes, which is given them at noon to swallow their allowance of cold bacon, they are not permitted to be a moment idle until it is too dark to see, and when the moon is full, they often times labor till the middle of the night. Upon leaving the fields, each one must attend to his respective chores. One feeds the mules, another the swine—another cuts the

wood, and so forth; besides the packing [of cotton] is all done by candlelight. Finally, at a late hour, they reach the quarters, sleepy and overcome with the long day's toil.

The work went on from dawn to dusk. Thus, the longer days of summer meant longer work hours. But masters found plenty for slaves to do in winter and on rainy days. Inside work was usually saved for a rainy day. In fact, the rules of proper plantation management called for a regular routine of work, twelve to fifteen hours a day, twelve months a year.

Slaves had Sunday off and usually, although not universally, Saturday afternoon. The time off was hardly idle. The slaves were expected to repair and clean their quarters and tend to their vegetable gardens, the yield of which supplemented the meager diet provided by the slave owner. Slaves usually got the major holidays off and a one-week "vacation" at Christmas.

The problem of the slave owner was to get the maximum amount of work from slaves, yet not overwork them. If slaves were driven long hours at backbreaking work and not given sufficient food and rest, they would become sick and exhausted. The slave owner knew slaves were human beings. There was a limit to how long and hard they could work. And a slave was valuable property, worth perhaps as much as two thousand dollars. The master hardly wanted to lose his property through overwork. To say the least, the planter was seldom successful in finding a happy medium between work and overwork.

The Threat of the Whip

There were two main ways to get work from slaves. One was known as the task system. Each slave was assigned a quota of work each day. When he finished and the work was checked, he was allowed the rest of the day off. In theory, at least, the task system gave the slave an incentive to work hard and well. But the system was not widely used. In the cotton, sugar, and hemp-growing areas there was an endless amount of work to do. The slave quickly learned that no matter how well he did his work, it wasn't well enough. So he quit trying. The only area where the task system was effective was in the rice areas, where the fields were smaller and work assignments were more clearly defined.

The most common method of obtaining productivity was the gang system. Twenty, thirty, or more slaves worked as a unit, each supervised by an overseer or driver. The overseer, frequently on horseback, supervised the gang, preventing lazy or careless work and driving the slaves to greater efforts.

The overseer used whatever methods he could to drive the slaves—verbal abuse, ridicule, striking the slave, or physically shoving him toward his work. But the most common method, by far, was the whip, which, more than anything else, was the in-

Humans as Property

In his book Slavery in America, *author Robert Liston emphasizes that the most dehumanizing aspect of slavery was the way in which slaves were treated as property rather than as persons.*

One reason slavery in America was so brutal was that the slave owner and the South in general knew that the slave was a human being. He was recognized under the law as a person. He was counted in the South's representation in the Congress of the United States. Laws were established for his protection, even though the laws were seldom enforced. He could not be worked more than fifteen hours a day. He could not be excessively mistreated. His owner was compelled by law to feed, clothe, house, and otherwise provide for his human needs. But many other laws attempted to thwart the slave's human faculties. He could not be taught to read and write. He could not travel or congregate with his friends for religious, social, or other purposes without permission. And often the presence of a white man was required. In short, much of the brutality of slavery lay in the fact that the slave owners knew the slaves were human but treated them as property.

Robert Liston, *Slavery in America: The History of Slavery.* New York: McGraw-Hill, 1970, p. 82.

strument that forced the slaves to work and punished wrongdo-ing. Indeed, the whip was the symbol of authority of the overseer. A visitor could always tell the overseer, even without seeing the color of his skin. He carried a whip.

The planters, always interested in productivity, tried other methods to get the slaves to work. They praised them. They bribed them with incentives of extra rations, or time off, or luxuries, such as a piece of calico cloth or a jar of molasses. But sooner or later virtually every slave owner came down to the whip. And there were many owners who were convinced that it was silly to bother with any other method.

By all accounts, the overseer was a big problem to the planter. He was the man in charge of production on the plantation, and pro-duction meant driving the slaves. A good overseer was rare. The overwhelming percentage of planters changed overseers every year or two, vainly hoping for a man who was less brutal and more competent to manage slaves. Masters set forth elaborate rules for overseers to follow, specifying the number of hours slaves were to be worked, various punishments to be meted out, slave rations, and much more. But the great difficulty planters had in finding over-seers indicates that the rules were seldom followed. The low pay, the great number of tasks to be done, the near impossibility of driv-ing slaves who didn't want to work, made the position of overseer far from an attractive one. Able men seldom wanted this job.

Assisting the overseer were one or more drivers. These were trusted slaves given the authority to use the whip upon their fellow slaves. As the name implies, they were to drive the slaves, whipping the slow, lazy, and careless. How did masters get slaves to whip other slaves? Simple. If they didn't whip, they were whipped.

It might be argued that this emphasis upon whipping is exag-gerated. Many slaves never felt the whip. Weeks would go by on plantations without the lash being applied. Yet it cannot be de-nied that the whip made slaves work. When not in use, the whip was a constant threat. Overseers and drivers carried it. Every slave had seen someone being whipped. He knew the consequences of not working. His apparent docility and enjoyment of his work was to a great extent a product of the whip.

The largest group of slaves, next to field hands, were domestic servants. Every master, even if his plantation was small, felt the need of at least one slave to personally wait upon him. The slaveholder's social status was derived as much from the size of his domestic staff as from the size of his plantation, the elegance of his big house, his bank accounts or flashy carriages.

The domestic slave had an easier life than the field hand. He did not toil fifteen hours in the hot sun. No one drove him with a whip, although many a maid or houseboy felt the sting of his master's or mistress's fury. The domestic had better food, clothing, and, when he lived in the mansion, housing. Yet he paid a price for it. He was constantly under the eye of the owner, expected to behave in a docile, servile manner. He was to ape the manner of white folks, yet he was seldom without awareness that he was a boy, a slave who had only a first name.

A Life of Squalor

What did the slaves receive in return for their toil? A favorite argument of the apologists for slavery was that slaves were better off economically than paid workers in the North. It was pointed out that most Northern workers labored a twelve-hour day in a factory. Child labor was common. The worker had to pay for housing, food, clothing, and medical care. If the worker was laid off or fired, he still had to pay all his expenses.

In contrast, the South argued, the slave had all his needs cared for. He had no need for money. The master provided housing, clothing, food, and medical care. He was never laid off or fired. When he grew old, he was cared for. By custom and by law, owners took care of slaves unable to work.

If the slave was paid in the form of total subsistence, rather than money, then he received very low pay. Most slaves lived in squalor, ate and dressed poorly, and died early deaths. There were exceptions. A few plantations provided subsistence equal to or even better than that of Northern workers. Olmsted described slave houses in Louisiana "as neat and well-made externally as the cottages usually provided by large manufacturing companies in New England." Some slave dwellings were well made, with plastered walls, floors, windows, and heat, but it was a lucky slave who got to live in them.

How well the slave shacks were built depended on the wealth of the owner, his charity toward his slaves, and how much he realized that housing affected the health of his slaves and thus their productivity. The typical slave quarters were usually a single or double row of buildings some distance from the mansion, but within view of the overseer's cottage. There were single or double units for the slave families, and dormitories for the unmarried slaves. . . .

If housing was bad, the food was deplorable. All that can be said in defense of slave owners is that they had virtually no knowledge of nutrition. The basic diet consisted of cornmeal and salt pork or bacon. The usual adult ration was a peck of meal and three or four pounds of pork a week per person. This was, at times, supplemented with sweet potatoes, peas, rice, syrup, and fruit. The slave could grow a few vegetables on his plot of land—if he wasn't too tired. Some slaves were permitted to fish and even occasionally to hunt. At Christmas the owner might provide a little coffee, cheese, or candy.

It was a rare slave who had adequate food. After all, he spent twelve or more hours at heavy labor and needed three thousand or more calories a day just to maintain his strength. Even when the food provided enough bulk to fill his stomach, he never had a balanced diet. Vitamin deficiencies and disease resulted.

Feeding the slaves was always a problem to the master. He was usually so bent on cultivating cotton or other money crops that he neglected to grow enough food to feed his slaves. He had to import grain and pork, and it was not always available. The shortage of food gave the owner another problem: stealing. Robbing the corncrib or smokehouse became a highly developed art among the slaves. . . .

Disease and Death

By modern standards, medical care for the slaves was nonexistent. A scourge of diseases was visited upon slaves each year, including smallpox, yellow fever, cholera, dysentery, tetanus (lockjaw), plus the more common diseases, such as scarlet fever and typhoid fever. The state of medicine in the first half of the nineteenth century was primitive, to say the least. Doctors generally treated all ailments by bleeding the patient or administering harsh laxatives.

Physicians perhaps caused as many deaths as diseases did.

Disease is no respecter of skin color. Whites as well as blacks were victims, and life expectancy was low for everyone. But the slave could expect a shorter life than the white person. The census of 1850 showed the average age for Negroes to be 21.5 at the time of death and 25.5 for whites. In 1860, the death rate for slaves was 1.8 and 1.2 for whites. In Mississippi, the life expectancy was only 17.5 for Negroes and 19.2 for whites. One plantation owner reported that of his nearly one hundred slaves, the oldest was only sixty-two and only five were over fifty. A Louisiana planter had 109 slaves, the oldest of whom was sixty-seven.

The infant mortality rate was astronomical. A South Carolina planter reported 111 slave births during an eleven-year period. Of these thirty-eight died before the age of one and fifteen more by age four. Mississippi reported 2,772 infant slave deaths in one period, and only 1,315 white infant deaths. In general, the slave infant death rate was double that of the white population.

Work Without Dignity

But it would be a gross mistake to assume that what made slavery in America so brutal were the toil and living conditions just described. Even today, as throughout history, a life of toil, hunger, and disease is the lot of most of the population of the world. Actually, enduring hard work and privation has always dignified man. Consider the pioneers, frontiersmen, homesteaders, and millions of immigrants who settled and built the United States. What made slavery so brutal in the United States is the simple fact that the slave did not win dignity from his toil and privation. Instead, he was systematically humiliated and dehumanized.

Viewpoint 4

"Some scholars . . . have tended to portray the material conditions of slave life too harshly."

The Harshness of Slave Life Has Been Exaggerated

William K. Scarborough

University of Southern Mississippi professor William K. Scarborough is the author of *The Overseer: Plantation Management in the Old South* and *Masters of the Big House: The Elite Slaveholders of the Mid–Nineteenth Century South.* In the following viewpoint, first published in 1976, Scarborough contends that some historians have depicted slave life in too harsh a manner. Scarborough agrees that slavery was deplorable and dehumanizing, but also notes that slave owners of the Old South had lived with the institution all their lives and did not see it as an evil. He cites evidence from the historical record to show that many masters treated their slaves with kindness and were mindful of slaves' health and well-being. For example, Scarborough notes that slaves were granted regular holidays, and on some plantations they received medical care and were allowed to earn money. He argues that on many plantations slaves were able to take complaints about working conditions directly to their mas-

William K. Scarborough, "Slavery—The White Man's Burden," *Perspectives and Irony in American Slavery*, edited by Harry P. Owens. Jackson: University Press of Mississippi, 1976. Copyright © 1976 by University Press of Mississippi. Reproduced by permission.

ter, and that many masters took their slaves' opinions into account in matters of plantation policy. Scarborough concludes that the limited freedoms that slaves received and the compassion with which they were treated were important to the stability of plantation society.

In many respects the blight of slavery constitutes one of the most lamentable chapters in the history of the American republic. For, more than any other institution in the two hundred years of our existence as a nation, it has served to divide our people and to tarnish the lofty principles upon which this country was founded. Indeed, even now the legacy of slavery continues to engender strife and bitterness.

Yet, there is another side to the ledger. Despite the debilitating influence of slavery—especially upon blacks—the plantation society of the Old South was not without its virtues. The export trade in southern staples played a vital role in the development of commerce and industry, not only in the United States but throughout the Western world. Moreover, the civilization of which slavery was an integral part spawned a remarkable galaxy of political leaders who, in large measure, laid the foundations of our democratic republic. It would be difficult to imagine the path which this nation would have traveled without the services of such slaveholders as George Mason, George Washington, Thomas Jefferson, James Madison, John Marshall, and Andrew Jackson—to name but a few of the most obvious. Subsequent generations, both white and black, have benefited from the monumental contributions which these men rendered to the American political system.

Historians have long been fascinated by the subject of slavery. It is doubtful whether any other facet of the American experience has been studied more assiduously nor claimed more of their time and talents. Apart from its manifest historical significance, there are several reasons for this perennial interest. To some scholars, especially non-southerners, it seems to have an almost exotic attraction, representing a society and culture totally alien to their own. To others it is seen as a vehicle by which to better understand and seek solutions to contemporary problems. There can be little doubt that much of the recent interest in slavery was sparked by the civil rights revolution, which induced blacks to embark upon the quest for a separate identity and caused many whites to seek a convenient scapegoat by which to expiate the guilt produced by more than three centuries of discrimination against black Americans.

Whatever the cause, the last two decades [1950s and 1960s] have witnessed the publication of a plethora of books and articles relating to the slave experience in America. Almost without exception, these writings have been of uncommonly high quality. Especially significant have been the efforts to eradicate racism from a depiction of the slave South and to view the institution of slavery from the perspective of those who endured its iniquities. . . .

However, despite the many advances, recent studies of slavery are not without their deficiencies. Understandably influenced by the civil rights crusade, some scholars, especially those writing in the 1950s, have tended to portray the material conditions of slave life too harshly. More recent writers, while conceding that the system was marked by a high degree of paternalism, seem constrained to view all acts of benevolence as either self-serving or motivated solely by considerations of economics or social control. Thus, although much progress has been made in clarifying the attitudes and personality types of the slaves, that progress has been at the expense of distorting the character and motivations of the masters. Consequently, I shall here attempt to view the institution of slavery from the perspective of the slaveholding class, especially the great planters, and in the process to respond to certain interpretations propounded in recent years by scholars of the slave South.

I hope that my subsequent remarks will not be misconstrued as constituting a defense of slavery or as betraying an insensitivity to the very real sufferings of black people under slavery. In emphasizing the paternalistic character of southern slavery, I do not mean to minimize the inherent inhumanity and brutality of depriving any individual of his personal freedom and his dignity as a human being. That, of course, is an inescapable and central feature of every slave system, and in the Old South it was compounded by the added ingredient of racism.

Slaveholders' Paternalism

Having admitted this, however, I think it is imperative to remember that slavery, in one form or another, had been a part of the human experience in the Western world since the beginning of recorded history. Antebellum southerners did not originate the institution of chattel slavery. Instead, they drifted into it, adopting it gradually, by custom—not step-by-step as a matter of deliberate choice, as Professor [Kenneth] Stampp has argued. Moreover, they were aided and abetted in its establishment by European merchants, Yankee slavetraders, and tribal chieftains in Africa. By the nineteenth century most white southerners had come to regard it as the foundation-stone of their socioeconomic system, as the right institution in the right place at the right time. However much we may deplore that judgment, we should not allow the moral outrage engendered by twentieth-century moral and ethical standards to color our interpretation of one of the most remarkable classes in American history, the planters of the slave South. . . .

Christian Compassion

The fact is, of course, that Christianity was a powerful factor in the lives of most antebellum southerners, both black and white. Although most southern whites saw no inherent incompatibility between Christian doctrine and the ownership of slaves, their diaries and letters reveal that many of them were devoutly religious and committed sincerely to the basic tenets of Christianity, at least as they understood them. Thus, it was a combination of Christian compassion and economic interest which produced near-unanimous agreement among planters that the welfare of their slaves was the paramount consideration. As one Mississippi slaveholder observed, no subject demanded more careful attention by the master than the proper treatment of his slaves, "by whose labor he lives, and for whose happiness and conduct he is responsible in the eyes of God."

In many respects the relationship between master and slave was analogous to that between a father and his children, as, indeed, the word "paternalism" implies. This view was expressed explicitly by Maunsel White when he wrote, "we view our Slaves almost in the same light we do our Children." The typical planter treated his

slaves with justice, humanity, and compassion; in return, he expected—indeed, demanded—obedience, loyalty, and good de-
portment. Just as the father was omnipotent in his own house-
hold, so too was the proprietor omnipotent within the realm of
the plantation. He had great power—indeed, the power of life and
death over his black wards—but in most cases he exercised that
power responsibly. For those not naturally disposed to govern in
such a manner, peer pressure was an important factor in enforc-
ing conformity to the norm. Those who earned the reputation of
being cruel masters usually incurred the odium of their neighbors
and suffered social ostracism. . . .

There is abundant evidence from the traditional sources to sustain the position that benevolent paternalism was practiced
widely, if not universally, in the slave South; that blacks were
treated pretty well as slaves, if not as human beings. . . .

Holidays, Slave Income, and Health Care

One of the standard privileges accorded southern slaves was freedom from labor on certain days of the year. Even by modern cri-
teria, the great planters were generous in their allocation of holidays. Sunday was customarily a day of rest except on Louisiana
sugar plantations during the grinding season. . . .

The most extended slave holiday, of course, was given at Christmas. Normally lasting from three to seven days and highlighted
by dancing, trips to town, gifts from the master, and at least one
sumptuous repast, it was always a gala occasion for plantation
blacks. Typical is the following entry from the plantation diary of
John Carmichael Jenkins, a Natchez planter: "Christmas day—we
shall not have any work done until beginning of New Year." Jenkins, an especially compassionate master, personally distributed
a gift to each of his slaves after the annual tree lighting on Christmas Eve at his Elgin plantation. Such gifts might include molasses,
whisky, tobacco, and calico for the adults or toys, candy, and fruit
for the children. One writer, who has made an intensive study of
the manuscript records of Natchez area planters, found no instance in which Christmas Day was not a holiday, nor any in
which slaves did not receive some sort of gift from their owners.
Moreover, she determined that the *average* length of the Christ-

mas holiday in that Deep South region was seven days. . . .

It was a standard practice on many plantations to permit slaves to raise poultry and to plant gardens on small plots of ground allocated to each family for that purpose. These privileges served two functions. First, they enabled the hands to supplement their basic fare of pork and corn meal, provided by the master, with such garden produce as peas, sweet potatoes, and pumpkins, as well as poultry and eggs. The effect was to add variety to the slave diet. But second, and perhaps more important, they provided a means by which the slaves could earn spending money with which to purchase coffee, sugar, tobacco products, Christmas presents, and other luxuries. A number of the major planters allowed their slaves to raise corn and hay on these individual plots. They then purchased these slave crops, often disbursing large sums of money for them. For example, in 1847 Valcour Aime paid his Negroes, which numbered just over 200, the startling amount of $1300 for their corn. Similarly, John C. Jenkins and Stephen Duncan regularly expended several hundred dollars each year for products raised by their hands. Such a system clearly served as a positive incentive for the slaves, allowing them a certain measure of personal freedom in purchasing consumer items and enabling black males to resist the emasculation process by providing more adequately for their families. . . .

There is ample evidence in the records of antebellum planters to support the judgment of William D. Postell that the health care accorded slaves "was no better and no worse than that of the populace as a whole for that period." Most slaveholders evinced genuine concern for the physical welfare of their Negroes. Minor ailments were usually treated by the master or overseer, but trained physicians were called in to diagnose and prescribe for more serious cases of slave illness. Expenditures for these professional services often contributed significantly to plantation overhead.

Discipline and Punishment

Thus far, I have emphasized primarily the benevolent aspects of the slave regime. There was, of course, another side—that of discipline and punishment. No matter how kindly and compassionate they might be under ordinary circumstances, all planters insisted upon discipline, order, and strict adherence to plantation rules and regulations. The best evidence of superior slave management—as the James River planter, Hill Carter, once observed—was the maintenance of "good discipline with little or no punishment." Unfortunately, this ideal was seldom realized. Rules were broken and the transgressors were punished. The slaveholders repeatedly enjoined their subordinates to be firm, impartial, and dispassionate in their chastisement of offending Negroes; or, as William J. Minor put it, to punish in a "gentlemanly manner." But, like the slave codes themselves, such injunctions were violated more often than they were observed.

Whipping, although distasteful to some, was the most common mode of punishment. Most planters limited the number of lashes which could be applied at any one time to a refractory slave. The most common maximum was fifty, but more indulgent masters specified much lower limits. Thus, Georgia planter George Jones Kollock and Plowden Weston, proprietor of a large South Carolina rice estate, prohibited punishments which exceeded ten and fifteen lashes, respectively. In order to diminish the likelihood of whippings being administered in a sudden passion, Weston further advised his overseers that it was "desirable to allow 24 hours to elapse between the discovery of the offense, and the punishment." Notwithstanding such safeguards, the sound of the whip and the cries of its victims reverberated across the Southland where it was the standard instrument of punishment on virtually all plantations. And if many southern slaves escaped its direct effect, all suffered from the omnipresent fear which even its occasional use inspired.

In the final analysis, the quality of life enjoyed by southern blacks depended, in large measure, upon the character of their individual masters. If there were many indulgent and compassionate slaveowners—men like Couper of Georgia, Jenkins of Mississippi, Polk and White of Louisiana, Allston and Weston of South Carolina—who exemplified to the highest degree those traits best described by the appellation "southern gentleman," there were also hard-headed businessmen like George Washington, who has been characterized by none other than Ulrich B. Phillips as "one of the least tolerant employers and masters who put themselves upon record," and downright sadists, such as Bennet H. Barrow and the first Wade Hampton. . . .

Balancing Power on the Plantation

Although I have here tried to view the institution of slavery from the perspective of the slaveholding class, I would be remiss if I did not consider briefly the role played by the slaves in defining the limits of the system. For, as Professors Blassingame and Genovese have so ably demonstrated, the latter exerted great influence in determining the guidelines under which they lived and labored. The master and his slaves were integral parts of the same community. Although the former, by law, exercised absolute power, the latter were constantly probing, continually challenging the limits of that authority—converting privileges into rights, helping to define policy, vetoing the selection of drivers and overseers. It was this arrangement that made life bearable for most plantation slaves; and knowing this, the planters readily acquiesced in the game.

However, for many masters, it was more than a game—more than just a device to promote harmony and order. A great many southern slaveholders earnestly solicited advice from their slaves and relied heavily upon both their individual and collective judgments as human beings. This is clearly discernible in the correspondence between plantation agents and their absentee employers. For example, in apprising Virginia planter John Hartwell Cocke of a request from a neighboring slave to marry a female servant on Cocke's Alabama plantation, the steward wrote: "Mr Borden's Boy (Washington) has a letter to me I learn, consenting for him to take a wife here. What say you? The servants don't wish it." Although the final decision obviously rested with Cocke, there is a clear implication that slave opinion carried considerable weight. Similarly, a Mississippi agent reporting on the progress of a new overseer informed his North Carolina employer that "from what I have seen and can learn from the negroes . . . [I think] he will do well. They are all satisfied with him." Once again, the judgment of the Negroes was solicited and reported to their master.

But the slaves did much more than merely offer their counsel on matters of policy. They made their greatest inroads upon the authoritarian character of the white power structure by deliberately exploiting natural antipathies among personnel in the managerial hierarchy—e.g., between driver and overseer, overseer and master. . . . There are countless examples of plantation slaves promoting such disharmony in order to ameliorate the psychological and material conditions of their daily lives.

Whenever a new overseer was employed, there was invariably a period of testing as the slaves sought to determine how much they could get away with under the new regime. Such an incident was reported by Louisiana planter Thomas Butler during a brief visit to his Grand Caillou sugar plantation.

> . . . some of the negroes are endeavouring to try the mettle & temper of the new overseer. Ned gave him some trouble & threatened not to live under his management. He is usually a quiet well disposed negro & may possibly have been put forward by some of the others. . . . I have told them all that the overseer would require nothing unreasonable from them & that they must submit to his authority. I am much pleased with his management but fear that he will have some difficulty when I leave. . . . I will however get Pierce [Butler's son] to ride down occasionally until Mr. Courquill is fairly established in authority.

If, after the initial period of testing, the Negroes were satisfied with their new manager, affairs usually proceeded smoothly and there were few disciplinary problems. In the contrary event, the disgruntled slaves might seek to oust the overseer by acts of massive disobedience or, if circumstances did not warrant such extreme action, to undermine his authority and mitigate the harshness of his regime by carrying complaints directly to the owner. . . .

Much to the consternation of plantation managers all over the South, most slaveholders permitted—and some explicitly directed—their Negroes to carry complaints . . . over the head of the overseer to the master. To comprehend why they did so, it is only necessary to understand the relative positions occupied by owner and manager under the slave system. As William Postell has pointed out, the overseer was "the symbol of the hardest features of slavery." It was he "who had to absorb the bitterness of bondage" as felt by those whose labors he directed. The planter, on the other hand, precisely because of the presence of a hired intermediary who could "take the heat," was enabled to assume the role of benevolent protector to the members of his black family. Thus, just as the policeman of today is often reviled as "pig" and the judge revered as an impartial arbiter, so too was the overseer an object of contempt and hatred while his employer commanded respect and often genuine affection.

In essence, then, the practice of affording southern slaves a direct avenue of appeal to their masters, or the latter's agents, acted as a safety valve, imparting flexibility to the system and alleviating frustrations which were potentially explosive. The point is well illustrated by a communication from an Alabama steward to his absentee employer in Virginia. Discussing the installation of a new overseer, he wrote: "Mr Carter speaks kindly & acts kindly toward them & I see they begin to feel it, but *it is important for* them *to Know I am ready* to *see them if necessary.*" For their part, the overseers could only protest and accept with resignation a situation over which they had little control. Thus, the veteran manager of Colonel John S. Preston's giant Houmas sugar estate recorded an infraction of plantation discipline in these terse words: "Jacob Ran off for nothing thinking Col Preston will be hear Soon and he will not be punished." In my judgment, the safety-valve concept explains, at least in part, why the vast majority of large slaveholders elected to retain the overseer system despite all its deficiencies and why insensitive planters, like Bennet Barrow, who dispensed with the services of white overseers had so many disciplinary problems.

Because of the sense of justice, honor, and noblesse oblige [obligation of honor] which induced many planters to treat their slaves with humanity and compassion, and because the system was flexible enough to allow the slaves a role in defining its limits, most southern Negroes were able to accommodate to the institution of chattel slavery.

Viewpoint 5

"One of the most immoral acts in the development of the United States was the enslavement of Africans, compounded by . . . refusal to make reparations for this crime."

The U.S. Government Should Pay Reparations to Blacks for the Harms Caused by Slavery

Ronald Walters

Ronald Walters is director of the African American Leadership Institute and a professor of government and politics at the University of Maryland. In the following viewpoint, he maintains that many of the problems facing black Americans today—including poverty and the breakdown of family structure—are due in large part to the subjugation of blacks under slavery, although many white Americans deny this connection. He further argues that previous attempts to undo the damage caused by slavery—including the efforts made during Reconstruction and the Civil

Ronald Walters, "Reparations for Slavery?: Let's Resolve the Inequity," *World & I*, vol. 15, April 2000, p. 18. Copyright © 2000 by News World Communications, Inc. Reproduced by permission.

Rights movement—have been halfhearted and ineffective. Walters believes that paying black Americans reparations for slavery would not only help blacks overcome the inequalities they face, but also symbolize the U.S. government's acknowledgment of the deep and lasting harms caused by slavery.

We are in a period of history where morality and ethics are emphasized as the primary ingredients of civil virtue. However, one of the most immoral acts in the development of the United States was the enslavement of Africans, compounded by (1) failure to acknowledge that the grandeur of this country was based, in substantial part, upon the monumental resources made possible by unpaid slave labor, and (2) refusal to make reparations for this crime. Most Americans have rejected the strength of America's slave heritage, and in so doing they devalue its contribution to the country's economic strength.

For example, the factory system emerged as an outgrowth of slavery when in 1790 Samuel Slater, an English immigrant who knew the secrets of English textile machinery, built a cotton-spinning mill at Pawtucket, Rhode Island, for a merchant named Moses Brown. This mill, with 72 spindles, became the first successful American factory. By the end of the War of 1812, hundreds of factories, with an estimated 130,000 spindles, were in operation, and by 1840 the number of spindles reached 2 million. Enslaved Africans in the South picked the cotton that fed these spindles and fueled the growth of the textile industry in New England.

This led to larger and more sophisticated manufacturing institutions known as corporations, until in 1865, at the end of the Civil War, a group of businessmen—including Frances Cabot Lowell, Nathan Appleton, and Patrick Tracy Jackson—formed the Boston Manufacturing Company, which later came to be known as the Boston Associates, in Waltham, Massachusetts. This was the first integrated factory in textiles; in other words, it performed every operation. In 1920 the company shifted operations to Lowell, Massachusetts, and became the Merrick Manufacturing Company, and in the 1920s and '30s it bought companies in Massachusetts and New Hampshire, making the manufacturing corporation an entrenched institution in America.

This failure to acknowledge the contribution of African Americans to the country's development fosters such cynicism and alienation that it prevents full faith in the institutionalized version of the American dream. Moreover, it contributes to the differential perceptions and interpretations of American life by blacks and whites, such as the O.J. murder verdict, the Los Angeles rebellions after the Rodney King verdict, and other racially charged incidents.

In 1998, we completed a cycle of national discussions on race known as "The Race Initiative," sponsored by President Clinton. However, this project failed to capture the imagination of the American people, partially because of the desperate attempt of conservatives to deny and suppress a discussion of the importance of the slave origins of American wealth and the country's debt to African Americans. Contrast this modern flight from responsibility to the words of William Pitt the Younger, head of state in 1807 when the English Parliament was passing legislation prohibiting the slave trade:

> I therefore congratulate this House, the country and the world that this great point is gained: that we may now consider this trade as having received its condemnation; that its sentence is sealed; that this curse of mankind is seen by the House in its true light; and that the greatest stigma on our national character which ever yet existed is about to be removed. And sir, (which is still more important) that mankind, I trust, in general, are now likely to be delivered from the greatest practical evil that ever has afflicted the human race—from the severest and most extensive calamity recorded in the history of the world!

Pitt did not temporize about the depth of the crime of slavery, as is generally the case in so many quarters today. Thus, when President Clinton, while traveling in Africa in March 1998, used language that appeared to broach an apology for slavery, by admitting that America had not always done the right thing by Africa, members of the Republican Party in Congress rose to denounce him immediately.

Linking Slavery to Modern Conditions

It is also currently fashionable to disconnect slavery from the modern patterns of disadvantage experienced by black Americans and to assert that they are due to the lack of "individual responsibility." Nevertheless, black people entered the role of citizens as an impoverished class. The distinguished black American intellectual W.E.B. DuBois noted in his study *The Philadelphia Negro* (1897) that "everywhere slavery was accompanied by pauperization" and that this condition of poverty prevented blacks from establishing a black middle class when wave upon wave of poor migrants from the South overwhelmed the fledgling black elite and defined poverty as the basic condition of the black urban ghetto. DuBois, Professors Kenneth Clark and William Wilson, and others have established a clear link between the "pauperization" of blacks and such social conditions as high crime rates, poor health, educational gaps, family social disorganization, high unemployment rates, poor neighborhoods, and substandard housing and other structures.

The reasons for these conditions, which characterize the black urban ghetto and the institutions within it even today, have been mystified, but slavery is responsible for having robbed black people of the economic resources necessary to acquire the cultural tools and institutions of the dominant group. These economic resources would have made possible the construction of schools and colleges that would have long ago closed any cultural gap in test scores and produced a large middle class of blacks that would have developed companies the equal of AT&T, IBM, or Morgan Stanley. This would have institutionalized a private economy that would have provided a substantial foundation for financial independence within the black community. The dimensions of this debt have attracted individuals such as Nobel Prize–winning Yale economist Boris Bittker, who analyzed this problem in his book *The Case for Black Reparations* as early as 1973.

The Longevity of Slavery

One reason given for denying reparations to African Americans and according them to Asian Americans is that the events that constituted a basis for the latter group occurred more recently, during World War II. However, it is one of the myths of American history and its historians that slavery ended in 1865. In fact, although legal slavery ended, in many places, especially in the South, the practice continued well into the twentieth century. The National Archives contains files of letters written in the 1920s, '30s, and '40s and sent to the NAACP [National Association for the Advancement of Colored People] by blacks who were still being held in slavery conditions on plantations in the South, still being forced to work without pay or to receive only symbolic wages, and still being brutalized. Then, debt slavery—where the sharecropping system held many former slaves in legal bondage, forcing them to work to pay mythical debts to landowners, was common. Finally, the prison system was expanded in the South and utilized to administer the convict-lease system, where blacks were convicted on petty or nonexistent crimes and leased out to work for merchants and plantation owners in slavery conditions. These situations were in many cases merely other forms of slavery, often worse than the original kind.

This system carried well into the twentieth century, as records of the Justice Department show. In a 1996 *Washington Post* article titled "Slavery Did Not End With the Civil War: One Man's Odyssey Into a Nation's Secret Shame," Len Cooper cites a newspaper story that described a Justice Department prosecution of the Dial brothers in Sumpter County, Alabama, in 1954 because they had held blacks in involuntary servitude. This means that the civil rights movement was the force that broke the final link to slavery. The fact that some blacks were held in slavery until after World War II and that cases of lynching also extended to that period refutes any proposition that slavery ended in 1865. This establishes a modern basis for reparations for the descendants of slaves as legitimate as that of any other group.

Government Responsibility

We also live in an era when there is much public dialogue about "individual responsibility," rather than the responsibility of government. Yet, in this case, there is both a rejection of individual responsibility for slavery—on the basis of longevity, recency of immigration, or other factors—and a reluctance to acknowledge the culpability of the state in administering the past slave status of African Americans. These have combined into the feeling that since neither individual nor government responsibility was possible, the pursuit of such a public policy was "unrealistic" and used ultimately, by both blacks and whites, to successfully evade an American dialogue about this issue. Real reparations, however, have been given to other groups. Slavery and the extermination of the Native American are the only truly American holocausts, but whereas the Native Americans have been given land and a system of government, however flawed, black Americans have not been compensated for slavery and certainly have not enjoyed benefits beyond those available to other American citizens. And while reparations have been informally refused blacks, Japanese-American internees during World War II received them. In fact, it is possible to argue that past attempts made to make amelioration for slavery have been dismantled before they could be implemented, or changed to advantage the majority, whether in the case of Reconstruction, civil rights, or even affirmative action.

I refer to the responsibility of government as the main authority figure in arranging recompense for slavery because at every stage individual Americans were permitted to practice slavery by writ of law, by each of the colonial territories even before there was a United States of America, certainly by the Constitutional Congress, and by successive acts of the Supreme Court, the Congress, and the state governments. So, as much as individuals are sensitive to the demand for reparations out of their own moral culpability for slavery, it is a basic responsibility of government. Similarly, it was the government—not the individual soldier who guarded the gates of the prison compounds or those civilians who lived in the Japanese Americans' confiscated homes—that paid Japanese reparations.

Material Recompense for the Crime of Slavery

There is a deep sensitivity among the descendants of slaves in America today that a substantial part of the social distance between them and white America was created by the process of enslavement. Despite the rampant economic growth, the structural distance in economic resources has been maintained in that blacks still have only one-tenth the wealth, more than twice the poverty rate, and double the unemployment rate of whites. This means that the failure to replace appropriated black economic resources as an "unrealistic" public policy is one of the powerful factors that results in the inability of both blacks and whites to "get beyond race," because the reluctant pace of resolving the inequality continues to place an emphasis on the fact that blacks in America are the only group expected to come all the way up the rough side of the mountain—in the most economically competitive society in the world—without the requisite resources to do so. The other factor, of course, is the persistence of racism in nearly every sector of American life, a fact that continues to transfer resources to whites, buttressed by the attempt to attribute the subordinate status of blacks to their lack of effort, or their natural inferiority, as rendered in such works as *The Bell Curve*, by Charles Murray and Richard Herrnstein.

So it is obvious that the past is prologue to the project of racial reconciliation in America, just as it is in South Africa, Australia, or wherever people have been dispossessed of their resources. To address this problem in this country, there must be an American dialogue that truly gives national legitimacy to the identity of black people as African Americans, an identity with equal force vested in both terms. At the height of the attempt to pass civil rights laws in the 1960s, those opposed argued that the key to full black participation in American life is not the passage of laws but social acceptance. The other side of this equation is that acceptance must also come from blacks, and its foundation begins with acknowledging the role of the dominant culture in (1) the crime of slavery, (2) the equal crime of pretending that the gap between Africans and others is a natural condition rather than a product of enslavement, and (3) the need to make material recompense for the unpaid labor of those enslaved.

In the famous picture of Washington crossing the Delaware River, there is a black man in the boat at the oars. His name was Prince Whipple, the son of a king in West Africa. He was sent to America for education but was instead enslaved by William Whipple, one of the signatories to the Declaration of Independence.

Whipple seconded Prince to be Washington's aide when Whipple went to war. As Whipple was leaving to join the fight for American independence as an officer, Prince Whipple was recorded to have said: "You are going to fight for your liberty, but I have none to fight for." Resolving the debt of slavery through reparations will help to combine what has been two different historical struggles for "freedom" into one.

Viewpoint 6

"The U.S. already made a mighty payment for the sin of slavery. It was called the Civil War."

The U.S. Government Should Not Pay Reparations to Blacks for the Harms Caused by Slavery

Karl Zinsmeister

Karl Zinsmeister is editor-in-chief of *American Enterprise* and has written opinion pieces for the *New York Times, Atlantic Monthly*, and the *Wall Street Journal*, among others. In the following viewpoint, he discusses why he feels the slavery-reparations movement—which holds that the federal government should make monetary payments to the black Americans for the harms caused by slavery—is misguided. Zinsmeister believes that the U.S. government made a mistake in not giving newly freed slaves land or other means of supporting themselves in the decade following the Civil War, but that any effort to

Karl Zinsmeister, "Has the Debt Been Paid?" *The American Enterprise*, vol. 12, July 2001, p. 4. Copyright © 2001 by American Enterprise Institute for Public Policy Research. Reproduced by permission of The American Enterprise, a magazine of Politics, Business, and Culture. On the web at www.TAEmag.com.

make up for that mistake in the twenty-first century would be fraught with practical and moral complications. Further, he asserts that the United States has made significant restitution to former slaves and their ancestors, primarily in the lives sacrificed in the Civil War, but also in the countless social support programs that local, state, and federal agencies have funded over the decades. Finally, Zinsmeister warns that the slavery-reparations movement could have a negative effect on race relations.

The activist campaign demanding payment of "slavery reparations" to today's black Americans probably strikes some readers as too far-fetched to take seriously. Better stop and look afresh. I myself realized that the concept had moved beyond faculty lounges, radical salons, and afrocentric pamphlets and into the realm of serious political struggle when I looked over the roster of a legal group convened to plot practical strategy for winning such compensation. It included not only DreamTeamer Johnny Cochran, Harvard Law School professor Charles Ogletree, and other ideologically predictable backers, but also one Richard J. Scruggs.

Scruggs is a white Mississippi trial lawyer with a single interest: causes which have a good chance of winning him lots of money. He is in the process of collecting billions of dollars (literally) for his part in the 1998 tobacco settlement. He is next trying to shake down HMOs and other unpopular businesses with the threat of legal action. He has his finger in dozens of other polemicized class-action suits. Scruggs also happens to be the brother-in-law of Republican Senator Trent Lott. When legal vultures like Scruggs, Dennis Sweet (hyper rich from Fen-phen diet pill suits), and class-action specialists Willie Gary and Alexander Pires begin to circle— they're all currently members of a "Reparations Assessment Group" which has both government and major corporations in its sights—some juicy carcass is usually about to be picked clean.

There are other hints that the push for payments to slave descendants is gaining momentum. Over the last year [2001], a dozen big-city councils have passed resolutions calling on the federal government to investigate reparations payments. Representative John Conyers has a bill in Congress that would require that. Representative Tony Hall, a white born-again Christian, is pushing a different proposal that would take up reparations; Republican congressman J.C. Watts has expressed guarded support. Quasi-conservative *Washington Post* columnist Charles Krauthammer wrote a column in April [2001] proposing to give African-American families a lump sum of $50,000 each. [Editor's note: As of July 2003 none of these measures has been enacted.]

Among blacks on the street, meanwhile, interest in reparations is shifting from pipe dream to popular demand. When I was in Dallas last year [2000] I heard hortatory ads by pro-reparations groups on black radio stations. Longstanding activist calls for black taxpayers to deduct "slavery credits" from their tax payments are being heeded by more African Americans. The IRS field office responsible for the region stretching just from northern Virginia to Delaware received 500 tax returns claiming such a credit (illegitimately) last year. "We're not talking about welfare. We're talking about back pay," is how the executive editor of *Ebony* magazine now describes reparations. Overall, polls show that most black Americans support having the government make slavery-restitution payments—in some surveys by considerably more than two-to-one.

This subject is not going to just quietly go away, as many Americans probably wish it would. The question must be faced. Are there merits to the case for slavery reparations?

Too Much Time Has Passed

I myself would characterize reparations as a good idea whose time has come and long since gone. In the years leading up to the Civil War there were various proposals for ending slavery through government payments. Lincoln called for federal compensation to states according to the number of slaves they emancipated. A portion of these payments could have been used to help the freed blacks establish themselves in a new life. Unfortunately, nothing came of this.

After financial dickering gave way to war, Union General William Sherman issued his famous field order decreeing that all freed slaves should be issued a mule and forty acres of land appropriated from plantation owners. But this was later countermanded. Much to the frustration of Republicans, new President Andrew Johnson vetoed such payments.

The result—a miserable one for blacks and for our nation—was that slaves, though liberated, were not provided any resources to help them transform themselves into self-supporting Americans. The "new Negro," Frederick Douglass wrote, "had neither money, property, nor friends. He was free from the old plantation, but he had nothing but the dusty road under his feet. . . . He was turned loose naked, hungry, and destitute to the open sky."

If cash had been spent as it should have been in the 1850s or '60s on reparations to slaves and indemnities to slaveowners, a terrible war might have been avoided. If money had been spent as it should have been during early Reconstruction to help the victims of slavery get themselves on their feet, a subsequent century of degrading poverty and segregation among blacks could have been mitigated.

But those opportunities were squandered, and there is no way to get them back. As black economist Walter Williams summarizes, "Slavery was a gross violation of human rights. Justice would demand that slave owners make compensatory reparation payments to slaves. Yet since both slaves and slave owners are no longer with us, compensation is beyond our reach."

Ah, but even with all the parties involved long dead, couldn't we make some sort of cleansing payment that would set things right? The answer is no. The two favorite models for slave reparations—payments to Holocaust victims and interned Japanese-Americans—are utterly different situations, because in those cases the injured parties and the injurers are still alive, and able to make direct restitution, one to another.

Meanwhile the identities of "slave" and "slaveholder" have blurred and melted away over the generations to the point where it is now impossible to say who would pay and who would receive in any accounting for slavery. There are plenty of Americans who have members of both groups in their family trees. The vast majority of us have neither—we weren't slaves; we weren't slave masters. Indeed, the majority of today's Americans descend from people who were not even in America when slavery was practiced.

And of the people who were here, a much larger number fought against slavery than practiced it.

It gets even messier than that. There were, for instance, approximately 12,000 black freemen living in the Confederacy who themselves owned slaves. Moreover, most of the individuals who came to America as slaves were dispatched into that state by other blacks in Africa. Who owes whom what in these cases?

The villains and the heroes of slavery have evaporated into the misty vapors of our past, and are now impossible to delineate clearly or bring to justice. Trying to pay slave reparations in our current decade would, as one observer puts it, mostly be a case of individuals who were never slaveholders giving money to people who were never slaves. A clear absurdity.

Political scientist Adolph Reed wrote recently in *The Progressive* that the only certain result of a reparations program would be to "produce a lively trade for genealogists, DNA testers, and other such quacks." Even Holocaust reparations—which are much simpler transfers directly to still-living victims—have turned extraordinarily unseemly and debasing. As Gabriel Schoenfeld noted recently in Commentary, "In the free-for-all to obtain Holocaust victims as clients . . . competing lawyers from the United States have barnstormed across Europe soliciting clients, publicly castigating each other, and privately maneuvering to oust their adversaries." If you think a subject as somber as slavery wouldn't be exploited (and ultimately decay into grasping, self-serving tawdriness) the second financial opportunism became possible, think again.

Considerable Restitution Has Already Been Made

American blacks would take little solace from simply being told it's too late for restitution, that practical impossibilities leave reparations for slavery out of reach. But that's not the whole story. The whole truth, which ought to offer black America real peace, is that the U.S. already made a mighty payment for the sin of slavery. It was called the Civil War.

I first decided to [write] on this subject almost exactly two years ago, when my hometown newspaper ran a Memorial Day ad honoring local men who had been killed in America's wars. The ad listed the names of 85 individuals who had died fighting the Civil War. I later did some research and discovered that the complete total for the three small towns that comprise our local school district was 105 killed.

The thing you need to know to put that figure in perspective is that our rural village [Cazenovia, NY] contains less than 3,000 people (and was not much different then). The surrounding towns add a couple thousand more. For our little community to have offered up 105 young men to be swallowed by the grave—most all of them between 18 and 29, the records show—was a great sacrifice.

Cazenovia's example was not a bit unusual. In all, more than 620,000 Americans died in the struggle to eliminate slavery. That is more than the number killed in all of our other wars combined. It amounted to a staggering 1.8 percent of our total population in 1865. That would be the equivalent of killing more than 5 million young Americans today.

The crux that defined and drove this ferocious fratricide was a determination to purge ourselves of slavery. It would be hard to overstate the pain and pathos involved in bringing that decision to its conclusion. President Lincoln's own family is an example: No fewer than seven of his brothers-in-law fought for the Confederacy; two were killed in battle. Yet Lincoln never wavered in doing what was right.

Though they are often now ignored, our nation is peppered with many powerful Civil War memorials. [There] . . . is a monument located down the road from my own home in New York state. Erected by a village of about 5,000 people, it hints at the magnitude of feeling which went into America's struggle to end enforced servitude. Our nation surely did run up a "debt" (as reparations advocates like Randall Robinson . . . like to put it) for allowing black bondage. But that bill was finally paid off, in blood.

And not only in blood. After tardily recognizing their error, Americans have tried to compensate for the historic harm visited upon African Americans. The massive infusions of money into income support, education, and special programs to benefit blacks that activists like Robinson are now calling for have already been offered up. Economist Walter Williams notes that over the last generation the American people have particularly targeted the black underclass with more than $6.1 trillion in antipoverty spending. Private and governmental agencies have tried to improve black socioeconomic status with measures ranging from affirmative action to massive philanthropic efforts. . . . American blacks have made remarkable progress.

But to the activists, this is not nearly enough. Perhaps there can never be enough done to placate them, because many are driven by an implacable sense of grievance more than a practical desire to see blacks flourish. In his book *The Debt*, Randall Robinson insists that blacks do not like America, and cannot be part of it. It's clear that is his own posture, and he actively urges other African Americans to share it. "You are owed," he tells his audience. "They did this to you."

This is a poisonous political path. It will be psychologically unhealthy for many blacks, and it is very likely to inspire a nasty backlash among other Americans. In his thorough article on Holocaust reparations (which, again, are far more solidly founded, because the actual victims are still with us) Gabriel Schoenfeld points out that renewed pressure on Europeans over Nazi-era atrocities has unleashed on that continent "a tide of anti-Semitic feeling unseen since the pre–World War II era." Aggressive reparations demands have created resentment both among intellectuals and on the streets, in the political arena as well as in social life.

Rehashing historical offenses is rarely constructive—especially since there are so many, extending in all directions and involving all races and groups. Despite the common references to slavery as America's "peculiar institution," the reality is that until the early nineteenth century there was hardly a country on earth without some kind of institutionalized slavery. One of my great-great-great-grandfathers, Mark Staggers, arrived here from England as a "bound boy"—in an indentured servitude which lasted for the rest of his childhood and much of his young adult years. My German ancestors were poor tenant farmers—the European equivalent of sharecroppers—who were repeatedly abused by Napoleon during the very years when U.S. slavery was at its peak.

Human bondage was not an American invention, it was a condition suffered by many people in many places across time. The northern U.S. states that outlawed slavery were among the first governments on the globe to do so. Rather than being some unique American stain, slavery was actually a commonplace sin, and almost six generations have now passed since it was outlawed throughout our land.

And balancing the ugliness of historical slavery in our country is the contemporary reality of enormous freedom and opportunity. Reparations activists will never say it so I will: Despite some harsh imperfections, America has, on the whole, been good to blacks, just as it has been good to other struggling groups who washed up on these shores. As economist Williams writes: "Most black Americans are middle class. And almost every black American's income is higher as a result of being born in the United States than in any country in Africa."

In the process of taming the wilderness, America's Anglo pioneers suffered heavily from human cruelty, natural disaster, disease, and deprivation. Even the most successful families sacrificed over and over. Of the 56 men who signed the Declaration of Independence to launch America, nine died of wounds or hardship during the Revolutionary War, five were captured or imprisoned, many had wives and children who were killed or imprisoned, 12 had their houses burned to the ground, 17 lost everything they owned, a number died bankrupt and in rags.

Those who followed bore other burdens. The Irish were felled in great numbers building our first canals and railways. Southern Europeans, Asians, Hispanics, and many other immigrants endured long indignities and drudging work helping to civilize a new land. The American society that sprang from the hardships endured by our ancestors now belongs to each of us—very much including blacks, who were some of our earliest arrivals.

There is no perfect accounting in the cosmos, and none of us sitting here in twenty-first-century America really did much to "deserve" the prosperity, pleasure, and long life that our country presently allows (to the great envy of the rest of humanity). We—including those of us who are black—are just lucky to be able to profit from those earlier sacrifices.

The American blessing is available today to every citizen, re-gardless of how rocky our family's entry into the country. There is no "us" or "them" to give manna, or take it, only a heavily in-terwoven "we" who share a common interest in the success of our one system. The ultimate compensation America offers current residents is a seat in the free-est and richest society yet created by man. It's the final payment, a gift to one and all.

CHAPTER 2

Slave Resistance and Rebellion

# Chapter Preface

One of the most significant slave rebellions for the United States took place outside its borders. In 1791, in the French Caribbean colony of Saint Domingue (now the nation of Haiti), tens of thousands of slaves, runaways, and free blacks began slaughtering whites in the northern settlements of Saint Domingue and burning the homes and property of slaveholders. The rebellion was the culmination of years of violent confrontations between black slaves and white slaveholders in the French colony, and it was also inspired in part by the French Revolution of 1789. The rebellion ended when it reached the port town of Cap Français, where whites were well armed and prepared to defend themselves. An estimated ten thousand blacks and two thousand whites were killed, and over one thousand plantations were sacked and razed. The rebellion at Cap Français, though unsuccessful, set in motion the events that led to the abolition of slavery in Saint Domingue in 1794 and eventually the Haitian revolution of 1803, from which Haiti emerged as the world's first free black republic.

The Haitian slave rebellion of 1791 inspired blacks and scared whites in the United States, especially in the South, where in some areas slaves outnumbered whites by a ratio of ten to one. However, the United States never experienced a slave rebellion nearly as large as Saint Domingue's. The largest slave rebellion within the United States came in 1831, when slave and lay preacher Nat Turner led sixty followers on an attack that killed approximately sixty whites, including Turner's owner and the owner's family. Local whites, along with the Virginia and North Carolina militias, soon crushed the rebellion. Turner was caught and hanged, and more than one hundred blacks were killed by vigilante groups in retribution.

Like the Haitian rebellion before it, Nat Turner's rebellion exacerbated whites' fear of slave rebellion and fueled the growing controversy over slavery. Black leaders in the North debated whether violent resistance to slavery was justified, and in the South some free blacks secretly urged further uprisings. The Virginia legislature debated whether to abolish slavery but instead voted to enact more restrictive laws against free blacks.

During the 1830s the most contentious debates about slave rebellion concerned whether such violence was justified and, among slaveholders, how it might be suppressed. Later generations would ask different questions, such as why the United States never experienced slave rebellions that were as frequent or as successful as those in other parts of the New World. These and other questions are explored in the following chapter.

Viewpoint 1

"You [slaves] are prisoners of war . . . and therefore, by all the rules of war, you have the fullest liberty to plunder, burn, and kill, as you may have occasion to do to promote your escape."

Resistance to Slavery Is Justified

Frederick Douglass et al.

Frederick Douglass was one of the foremost black leaders of his time. Born a slave in 1818 in Maryland, he escaped in 1838 and became a noted abolitionist speaker for William Lloyd Garrison's Massachusetts Anti-Slavery Society. His autobiography *The Narrative Life of Frederick Douglass* was first published in 1845. In 1847 he began publishing his own abolitionist newspaper, the *North Star*.

On August 21, 1850, Douglass presided at a convention in Cazenovia, New York, known as the Fugitive Slave Convention. More than two thousand people attended, of whom about thirty were fugitives. The convention drafted an open letter to the slaves of America, portions of which are excerpted below. The letter openly encourages slaves to seek escape, and, if necessary, to take up arms against their masters, likening slaveholders to tyrants and slaves to prisoners of war. The letter was drafted just

Frederick Douglass et al., "A Letter to the American Slaves from Those Who Have Fled from American Society," *Frederick Douglass: Selected Speeches and Writings*, edited by Philip S. Foner. Chicago: Lawrence Hill Books, 1999.

four weeks before the enactment of the Fugitive Slave Law, which required Northern law enforcement officials to arrest runaway slaves and return them to their owners.

A fflicted and Beloved Brothers:
The meeting which sends you this letter, is a meeting of runaway slaves. We thought it well, that they, who had once suffered, as you still suffer, that they, who had once drunk of that bitterest of all bitter cups, which you are still compelled to drink of, should come together for the purpose of making a communication to you.

The chief object of this meeting is, to tell you what circumstances we find ourselves in—that, so you may be able to judge for yourselves, whether the prize we have obtained is worth the peril of the attempt to obtain it.

The heartless pirates, who compelled us to call them "master," sought to persuade us, as such pirates seek to persuade you, that the condition of those, who escape from their clutches, is thereby made worse, instead of better. We confess, that we had our fears, that this might be so. Indeed, so great was our ignorance, that we could not be sure that the abolitionists were not the friends, which our masters represented them to be. When they told us, that the abolitionists, could they lay hands upon us would buy and sell us, we could not certainly know, that they spoke falsely; and when they told us, that abolitionists are in the habit of skinning the black man for leather, and of regaling their cannibalism on his flesh, even such enormities seemed to us to be possible. But owing to the happy change in our circumstances, we are not as ignorant and credulous now, as we once were; and if we did not know it before, we know it now, that slaveholders are as great liars, as they are great tyrants.

Life in the North

The abolitionists act the part of friends and brothers to us; and our only complaint against them is, that there are so few of them. The abolitionists, on whom it is safe to rely, are, almost all of them, members of the American Anti-Slavery Society, or of the Liberty Party. There are other abolitionists: but most of them are grossly inconsistent; and, hence, not entirely trustworthy abolitionists. So inconsistent are they, as to vote for anti-abolitionists for civil rulers, and to acknowledge the obligation of laws, which they themselves interpret to be pro-slavery.

We get wages for our labor. We have schools for our children. We have opportunities to hear and to learn to read the Bible— that blessed book, which is all for freedom, notwithstanding the lying slaveholders who say it is all for slavery. Some of us take part in the election of civil rulers. Indeed, but for the priests and politicians, the influence of most of whom is against us, our condition would be every way eligible. . . .

Including our children, we number in Canada, at least, twenty thousand. The total of our population in the free States far exceeds this. Nevertheless, we are poor, we can do little more to promote your deliverance than pray for it to the God of the oppressed. We will do what we can to supply you with pocket compasses. In dark nights, when his good guiding star is hidden from the flying slave, a pocket compass greatly facilitates his exodus. Candor requires the admission, that some of us would not furnish them, if we could; for some of us have become nonresistants [pacifists], and have discarded the use of these weapons: and would say to you: "love your enemies; do good to them, which hate you; bless them that curse you; and pray for them, which despitefully use you." Such of us would be glad to be able to say, that all the colored men of the North are nonresistants. But, in point of fact, it is only a handful of them, who are. When the insurrection of the Southern slaves shall take place, as take place it will unless speedily prevented by voluntary emancipation, the great majority of the colored men of the North, however much to the grief of any of us, will be found by your side, with deepstored and long-accumulated revenge in their hearts, and with death-dealing weapons in their hands. It is not to be disguised, that a colored man is as much disposed, as a white man, to resist, even unto death, those who oppress him. The colored American, for the sake of relieving his colored brethren, would no more hesitate to shoot an American slaveholder, than would a white

American, for the sake of delivering his white brother, hesitate to shoot an Algerine slaveholder. The State motto of Virginia: "Death to Tyrants;" is as well the black man's, as the white man's motto. We tell you these things not to encourage, or justify, your resort to physical force; but, simply, that you may know, be it to your joy or sorrow to know it, what your Northern colored brethren are, in these important respects. This truth you are en-

Slaves Are Too Servile

David Walker was a free black who in 1829 published a pamphlet called Appeal, in Four Articles *that decried slavery and exhorted slaves to resist their masters. He died under mysterious circumstances a year later. The pamphlet, the first extended political tract written by an African American, was attacked by Southerners who attempted to limit its distribution. Many slaveholders also blamed it for helping instigate the 1831 Nat Turner insurrection, a slave uprising in Southampton, Virginia, in which approximately sixty whites were killed.*

They (the whites) know well, if we are *men*—and there is a secret monitor in their hearts which tells them we are—they know, I say, if we *are* men, and see them treating us in the manner they do, that there can be nothing in our hearts but death alone, for them, notwithstanding we may appear cheerful, when we see them murdering our dear mothers and wives, because we cannot help ourselves. Man, in all ages and all nations of the earth, is the same. Man is a peculiar creature—he is the image of his God, though he may be subjected to the most wretched condition upon earth, yet the spirit and feeling which constitute the creature, man, can never be entirely erased from his breast, because the God who made him after his own image, planted it in his heart; he cannot get rid of it. The whites knowing this, they do not know what to do; they know that they have done us so much injury, they are afraid that we, being men, and not brutes, will retaliate, and woe will be to them;

titled to know, however the knowledge of it may affect you, and however you may act, in view of it.

The Use of Force to Achieve Freedom

We have said, that some of us are non-resistants. But, while such would dissuade you from all violence toward the slaveholder, let it not be supposed, that they regard it as guiltier than those strifes,

---

therefore, that dreadful fear, together with an avaricious spirit, and the natural love in them, to be called masters, (which term will yet honour them with to their sorrow) bring them to the resolve that they will keep us in ignorance and wretchedness, as long as they possibly can, and make the best of their time, while it lasts. Consequently they, themselves, (and not us) render themselves our natural enemies, by treating us so cruel. . . . We can help ourselves; for, if we lay aside abject servility, and be determined to act like men, and not brutes—the murderers among the whites would be afraid to show their cruel heads. But O, my God!—in sorrow I must say it, that my colour, all over the world, have a mean [abject], servile spirit. They yield in a moment to the whites, let them be right or wrong—the reason they are able to keep their feet on our throats. Oh! my coloured brethren, all over the world, when shall we arise from this death-like apathy?—And be men!! You will notice, if ever we become men, (I mean *respectable* men, such as other people are,) we must exert ourselves to the full. . . . Here now, in the Southern and Western sections of this country, there are at least three coloured persons for one white, why is it, that those few weak, good-for-nothing whites, are able to keep so many able men, one of whom, can put to flight a dozen whites, in wretchedness and misery?

David Walker's Appeal, in Four Articles: Together with a Preamble to the Coloured Citizens of the World, but in Particular, and Very Expressly, to Those of the United States of America, revised edition with an introduction by Sean Wilentz. New York: Hill and Wang, 1995.

which even good men are wont to justify. If the American revolutionists had excuse for shedding but one drop of blood, then have the American slaves excuse for making blood to flow "even unto the horse-bridles."

Numerous as are the escapes from slavery, they would be far more so, were you not embarrassed by your misinterpretations of the rights of property. You hesitate to take even the dullest of your master's horses—whereas it is your duty to take the fleetest. Your consciences suggest doubts, whether in quitting your bondage, you are at liberty to put in your packs what you need of food and clothing. But were you better informed, you would not scruple to break your master's locks, and take all their money. You are taught to respect the rights of property. But, no such right belongs to the slaveholder. His right to property is but the robber-right. In every slaveholding community, the rights of property all center in them, whose coerced and unrequited toil has created the wealth in which their oppressors riot. Moreover, if your oppressors have rights of property, you, at least, are exempt from all obligations to respect them. For you are prisoners of war, in an enemy's country—of a war, too, that is unrivalled for its injustice, cruelty, meanness—and therefore, by all the rules of war, you have the fullest liberty to plunder, burn, and kill, as you may have occasion to do to promote your escape. . . .

We cannot forget you, brethren, for we know your sufferings and we know your sufferings because we know from experience, what it is to be an American slave. So galling was our bondage, that, to escape from it, we suffered the loss of all things, and braved every peril, and endured every hardship. Some of us left parents, some wives, some children. Some of us were wounded with guns and dogs, as we fled. Some of us, to make good our escape, suffered ourselves to be nailed up in boxes, and to pass for merchandise. Some of us secreted ourselves in the suffocating holds of ships. Nothing was so dreadful to us, as slavery; and hence, it is almost literally true, that we dreaded nothing, which could befall us, in our attempt to get clear of it. Our condition could be made no worse, for we were already in the lowest depths of earthly woe. Even should we be overtaken, and resubjected to slavery, this would be but to return to our old sufferings and sorrows and should death itself prove to be the price of our endeavor after freedom, what would that be but a welcome release to men, who had, all their lifetime, been killed every day, and "killed all the day long.". . .

Brethren, our last word to you is to bid you be of good cheer, and not to despair of your deliverance. Do not abandon your-selves, as have many thousands of American slaves, to the crime of suicide. Live! live to escape from slavery, live to serve God! Live till He shall Himself call you into eternity! Be prayerful—be brave—be hopeful. "Lift up your heads, for your redemption draweth nigh."

Viewpoint 2

"I am certain that while we are slaves, it is our duty to obey our masters, in all their lawful commands."

Resistance to Slavery Is Not Justified

Jupiter Hammon

Jupiter Hammon was born in the early 1700s as a slave to a wealthy New York merchant family. He spent his lifetime in slavery as a trusted house servant, and evidently had a special status. He developed a superior command of the English language and, a devout convert to Christianity, preached and wrote religious poetry. Hammon was the first black to be published in America, with eight published pieces over the course of his life, all of them directed at a primarily black audience.

The following viewpoint is excerpted from *An Address to the Negroes of the State of New York*, a speech delivered before the African Society in New York City in 1786, and published in 1787. Hammon counsels slaves to be obedient to their masters and to concentrate on gaining freedom through religion rather than rebellion. Historians and literary critics have generally criticized the submissive and subservient stance that Hammon takes in this and other writings, but more recent scholars have suggested that Hammon believed that blacks could, like he had done, gain more by embracing white culture than they could by resisting slavery.

Jupiter Hammon, address before the African Society, New York, 1786.

When I am writing to you with a design to say something to you for your good, and with a view to promote your happiness, I can with truth and sincerity join with the apostle Paul, when speaking of his own nation the Jews, and say: "*That I have great heaviness and continual sorrow in my heart for my brethren, my kinsmen according to the flesh.*" Yes my dear brethren, when I think of you, which is very often, and of the poor, despised and miserable state you are in, as to the things of this world, and when I think of your ignorance and stupidity, and the great wickedness of the most of you, I am pained to the heart. It is at times, almost too much for human nature to bear, and I am obliged to turn my thoughts from the subject or endeavour to still my mind, by considering that it is permitted thus to be, by that God who governs all things, who setteth up one and pulleth down another. While I have been thinking on this subject, I have frequently had great struggles in my own mind, and have been at a loss to know what to do. I have wanted exceedingly to say something to you, to call upon you with the tenderness of a father and friend, and to give you the last, and I may say dying advice, of an old man, who wishes your best good in this world, and in the world to come. But while I have had such desires, a sense of my own ignorance, and unfitness to teach others, has frequently discouraged me from attempting to say any thing to you; yet when I thought of your situation, I could not rest easy.

When I was at Hartford in Connecticut, where I lived during the war, I published several pieces which were well received, not only by those of my own colour, but by a number of the white people, who thought they might do good among their servants. This is one consideration, among others, that emboldens me now to publish what I have written to you. Another is, I think you will be more likely to listen to what is said, when you know it comes from a negro, one of your own nation and colour, and therefore can have no interest in deceiving you, or in saying any thing to you, but what he really thinks is your interest, and duty to comply with. My age, I think, gives me some right to speak to you, and reason to expect you will hearken to my advice. I am now upwards of seventy years old, and cannot expect, though I am well, and able to do almost any kind of business, to live much longer. I have passed the common bounds set for man, and must soon go the way of all the earth. I have had more experience in the world than the most of you, and I have seen a great deal of the vanity and wickedness of it, I have great reason to be thankful that my lot has been so much better than most slaves have had. I suppose I have had more advantages and privileges than most of you, who are slaves, have ever known, and I believe more than many white people have enjoyed, for which I desire to bless God, and pray that he may bless those who have given them to me. I do not, my dear friends, say these things about myself, to make you think that I am wiser or better than others; but that you might hearken, without prejudice, to what I have to say to you on the following particulars.

Obedience

1st. Respecting obedience to masters.—Now whether it is right, and lawful, in the sight of God, for them to make slaves of us or not. I am certain that while we are slaves, it is our duty to obey our masters, in all their lawful commands, and mind them unless we are bid to do that which we know to be sin, or forbidden in God's word. The apostle Paul says: "Servants be obedient to them that are your masters according to the flesh, with fear and trembling in singleness in your heart as unto Christ: Not with eye service, as men pleasers, but as the servants of Christ doing the will of God from the heart: With good will doing service to the Lord, and not to men: Knowing that whatever thing a man doeth the same shall he receive of the Lord, whether he be bond or free."—Here is a plain command of God for us to obey our masters. It may seem hard for us, if we think our masters wrong in holding us slaves, to obey in all things, but who of us dare dispute with God! He has commanded us to obey, and we ought to do it cheerfully, and freely. This should be done by us, not only because God commands, but because our own peace and comfort depend upon it. As we depend upon our masters, for what we eat and drink and wear, and for all our comfortable things in this world, we cannot be happy, unless we please them. This we cannot do without obeying them freely, without muttering or finding fault. If a servant strives to please his master and studies and takes pains to do it, I believe there are but few masters who would use such a servant cruelly. Good servants frequently make good masters. If your master is really hard, unreasonable and cruel, there is no way so likely for you to convince him of it, as always to obey his commands, and try to serve him, and take care of his interest, and try to promote it all in your power. If you are proud and stubborn and always finding fault, your master will think the fault lies wholly on your side; but if you are humble, and meek, and bear all things patiently, your master may think he is wrong; if he does not, his neighbours will be apt to see it, and will befriend you, and try to alter his conduct. If this does not do, you must cry to him, who has the hearts of all men in his hands, and turneth them as the rivers of waters are turned.

Honesty

2d. The particular I would mention, is honesty and faithfulness.

You must suffer me now to deal plainly with you, my dear brethren, for I do not mean to flatter, or omit speaking the truth, whether it is for you, or against you. How many of you are there who allow yourselves in stealing from your masters. It is very wicked for you not to take care of your masters goods, but how much worse is it to pilfer and steal from them, whenever you think you shall not be found out. This you must know is very wicked and provoking to God. There are none of you so ignorant, but that you must know that this is wrong. Though you may try to excuse yourselves, by saying that your masters are unjust to you, and though you may try to quiet your consciences in this way, yet if you are honest in owning the truth, you must think it is as wicked, and on some accounts more wicked, to steal from your masters, than from others.

We cannot certainly, have any excuse either for taking any thing that belongs to our masters, without their leave, or for being unfaithful in their business. It is our duty to be faithful, *not with eye service as men pleasers*. We have no right to stay when we are sent on errands, any longer than to do the business we were sent upon. All the time spent idly, is spent wickedly, and is unfaithfulness to our masters. In these things I must say, that I think many of you are guilty. I know that many of you endeavour to excuse yourselves, and say, that you have nothing that you can call your own, and that you are under great temptations to be unfaithful and take from your masters. But this will not do, God will certainly punish you for stealing and for being unfaithful. All that we have to mind is our own duty. If God has put us in bad circumstances, that is not our fault, and he will not punish us for it. If any are wicked in keeping us so, we cannot help it, they must answer to God for it. Nothing will serve as an excuse to us for not doing our duty. The same God will judge both them and us. Pray then my dear friends, fear to offend in this way, but be faithful to God, to your masters, and to your own souls.

The next thing I would mention, and warn you against, is profaneness. This you know is forbidden by God. Christ tells us: "swear not at all," and again it is said, "thou shalt not take the name of the Lord thy God in vain, for the Lord will not hold him guiltless, that taketh his name in vain." Now, though the great God has forbidden it, yet how dreadfully profane are many, and I don't know but I may say the most of you? How common is it to hear you take the terrible and awful name of the great God in vain?— To swear by it, and by Jesus Christ, his Son—How common is it to hear you wish damnation to your companions, and to your own souls—and to sport with the name of Heaven and Hell, as if there were no such places for you to hope for, or to fear. Oh my friends, be warned to forsake this dreadful sin of profaneness. Pray my dear friends, believe and realize, that there is a God—that he is great and terrible beyond what you can think—that he keeps you in life every moment—and that he can send you to that awful Hell, that you laugh at, in an instant, and confine you there forever, and that he will certainly do it, if you do not repent. . . .

Murder Is Wicked

Some of you excuse yourselves, may plead the example of others, and say that you hear a great many white people, who know more, than such poor ignorant negroes, as you are, and some who are rich and great gentlemen, swear, and talk profanely, and some of you may say this of your masters, and say no more than is true. But all this is not a sufficient excuse for you. You know that murder is wicked. If you saw your master kill a man, do you suppose this would be any excuse for you, if you should commit the same crime? You must know it would not; nor will your hearing him curse and swear, and take the name of God in vain, or any other man, be he ever so great or rich, excuse you. God is greater than all other beings, and him we are bound to obey. To him we must give an account for every idle word that we speak. He will bring us all, rich and poor, white and black, to his judgment seat. If we are found among those who *feared his name* and *trembled at his word*, we shall be called good and faithful servants. Our slavery will be at an end, and though ever so mean, low, and despised in this world, we shall sit with God in his kingdom as Kings and Priests, and rejoice forever, and ever. Do not then my dear friends, take God's holy name in vain, or speak profanely in any way. Let not the example of others lead you into the sin, but reverence and fear that *great and fearful name, the Lord our God*.

I might now caution you against other sins to which you are exposed, but as I meant only to mention those you were exposed to, more than others, by your being slaves, I will conclude what I have to say to you, by advising you to become religious, and to make religion the great business of your lives.

True Liberty

Now I acknowledge that liberty is a great thing, and worth seeking for, if we can get it honestly, and by our good conduct prevail on our masters to set us free. Though for my own part I do not wish to be free: yet I should be glad, if others, especially the young negroes were to be free, for many of us who are grown up slaves, and have always had masters to take care of us, should hardly know how to take care of ourselves; and it may be more for our own comfort to remain as we are. That liberty is a great thing we may know from our own feelings, and we may likewise judge so from the conduct of the white people, in the late war. How much money has been spent, and how many lives have been lost, to defend their liberty. I must say that I have hoped that God would open their eyes, when they were so much engaged for liberty, to think of the state of the poor blacks, and to pity us. He has done it in some measure, and has raised us up many friends, for which we have reason to be thankful, and to hope in his mercy. What may be done further, he only knows, for *known unto God are all his ways from the beginning.* But this my dear brethren is by no means, the greatest thing we have to be concerned about. Getting our liberty in this world, is nothing to having the liberty of the children of God. Now the Bible tells us that we are all by nature, sinners, that we are slaves to sin and satan, and that unless we are converted, or born again, we must be miserable forever. Christ says, except a man be born again, he cannot see the kingdom of God, and all that do not see the kingdom of God, must be in the kingdom of darkness. There are but two places where all go after death, white and black, rich and poor; those places are heaven and hell. . . .

We live so little time in this world, that it is no matter how wretched and miserable we are, if it prepares us for heaven. What is forty, fifty, or sixty years, when compared to eternity. When thousands and millions of years have rolled away, this eternity will be no nigher coming to an end. Oh how glorious is an eternal life of happiness! and how dreadful, an eternity of misery. Those of us who have had religious masters, and have been taught to read the Bible, and have been brought by their example and teaching to a sense of divine things, how happy shall we be to meet them in heaven, where we shall join them in praising God forever. But if any of us have had such masters, and have yet lived and died wicked, how will it add to our misery to think of our folly. If any of us, who have wicked and profane masters should become religious, how will our estates be changed in another world. Oh my friends, let me intreat of you to think on these things, and to live as if you believed them true. If you become christians, you will have reason to bless God forever, that you have been brought into a land where you have heard the gospel, though you have been slaves. If we should ever get to heaven, we shall find nobody to reproach us for being black, or for being slaves. Let me beg of you my dear African brethren, to think very little of your bondage in this life, for your thinking of it will do you no good. If God designs to set us free, he will do it, in his own time, and way; but think of your bondage to sin and satan, and do not rest, until you are delivered from it.

Viewpoint 3

"The effort to prove that slaves did it all: accomplished their own redemption and were the 'commanding' force in what came to be known as the Underground Railroad is . . . inaccurate."

The Underground Railroad Aided Many Runaway Slaves

Louis Filler

Historian and Antioch College professor Louis Filler is the author of several books on slavery, including *Crusade Against Slavery: Friends, Foes, and Reforms, 1820–1860* and *The Rise and Fall of Slavery in America*, from which the following selection is excerpted. In it, Filler discusses the significance of runaway slaves, and the Fugitive Slave Act of 1793, designed to ensure their return to bondage. Filler writes that while many slaves escaped by relying on their own courage and ingenuity, countless others received aid from the Underground Railroad—a semi-secret network of free blacks and white abolitionists in the North and South who helped provide runaways with transportation and shelter on their journey to the North. Filler emphasizes the role of whites in the Underground Railroad, discussing how white participation in defying the slavery system strengthened abolitionist sentiment throughout the North.

During the 1830–1860 era, fugitive slaves accumulated a literature and lore of their own. Some were famous as cases, rather than individuals. The *Prigg Case* (1842) referred to the attorney for a slave owner, not to Margaret Morgan, a runaway slave who had fled from Maryland to Pennsylvania, and whose forcible return to slavery tested a Pennsylvania law making it illegal to carry a Negro out of the state for purposes of enslavement. The *Latimer Case* of the same year did refer to a runaway slave, George Latimer, seized in Boston for return to Norfolk, Virginia. The case caused severe excitement in Boston, and publication of a daily paper, *The Latimer Journal and North Star*. With Latimer in prison and abolitionists considering desperate actions for freeing him, the owner agreed to payment of four hundred dollars in exchange for dropping his suit.

The Fugitive Slave Law

The Constitution had provided for the return of fugitive slaves. It had not been specific in describing individual cases and conditions affected, and a national law covering such particulars had been demanded. Such was provided in 1793. This first Fugitive Slave Law was partial to the master; for example, it did not stipulate a trial by jury for alleged runaways. On the other hand, although the law supported the master's right to retrieve a fugitive slave, it placed no significant duties on other citizens to help him in his quest. Over the years this fact caused discontent among slaveholders who had reason to know that northern employers—whether sympathetic to abolition, or not—had been glad to assimilate their runaways into the free labor market. South-side petitions for a stronger fugitive slave law failed, and the issue became part of the developing national debate.

Northern whites had a limited interest in the Negro minority, but they nourished an increasing concern for liberty. Abolitionists publicized the fact that the weak defenses set up for harassed blacks could result in tragedy for whites. A profession of *slave-*

catchers had developed which brought to the fore hard and tenacious men, eager to collect rewards, and not too scrupulous about how they might be gained. Certified cases of the kidnapping of free Negroes on the pretext that they were runaways caused unease that the same snare might victimize whites as well, either directly, or because of weakened constitutional safeguards for individuals in general.

Fugitive slaves were mainly a product of the Border States, and contrived to make their way from Maryland and Delaware, Kentucky and Missouri, and also from Virginia. This state not only led into Maryland and Delaware, but also bordered on the Ohio River. Fugitives adopted many modes for finding their way to free states. They followed the North Star. If literate and resourceful, they carried false papers or messages. Sometimes they passed themselves off as free Negroes, or, if complexion permitted, as white. Frederick Douglass, greatest Negro of his generation, escaped by railroad from Maryland to New York by way of Philadelphia in 1838 by the desperate ruse of utilizing the seaman's papers of a free Negro. Harriet Tubman, "the Moses of her people," not only fled Maryland for Pennsylvania with nothing but wit and steely courage to guide her, but became all but legendary by returning a number of times to lead other slaves out of bondage. Henry "Box" Brown, a Richmond, Virginia slave attained fame by having himself boxed and shipped to Philadelphia. William and Ellen Craft were also nationally known, she of light complexion for having arrayed herself in male attire and passed as a planter, he, the dark-skinned one, for having accompanied her as a body-servant. They made their way through Georgia, South Carolina, Virginia, and Maryland, before reaching Philadelphia and freedom.

And so many others who used opportunity and determination in their bids for freedom. Douglass believed many more could have escaped, had they been willing to leave families and friends without hope of reunion. Some efforts ended in tragedy. Margaret Garner shook the North as much as did any slave when, following her family's flight from Kentucky to Ohio, and their capture, she strove to kill all her children. She did succeed in killing one, before being returned to Kentucky. En route by boat, she attempted suicide with another. She was then sold and lost farther south.

The Underground Railroad

Nevertheless, the effort to prove that slaves did it all: accomplished their own redemption and were the "commanding" force in what came to be known as the Underground Railroad is badly advised and inaccurate. It does not dignify Negro lore, as intended, but merely separates it from the great stream of human American experience which was inevitably dominated by the overwhelming majority of white people, North and South, all of whom, in different groups suffered their own agonies and adjustments and sank them into the American tradition. Slaves by themselves could have done little. It became a major goal of slavery partisans to implicate, by threats or appeals to reason, the entire North in the maintenance of slaveholder's prerogatives. Had this been achieved, the fugitive slave would have become a mere incident in the daily round of the Republic, readily controlled by an effective Fugitive Slave Law.

Dedicated white men throughout the North refused to accept this scheme for ignoring moral issues and brushing off the shadow of civil war which haunted the nation throughout the period. Famous names among aiders and abettors of fugitive slaves emerged to inspire others with their courage and resourcefulness. Rev. Charles T. Torrey, "father of the underground railroad," may have helped some four hundred Negroes to freedom before being apprehended, prosecuted, and committed in 1846 to the penitentiary in Maryland, where he died. Levi Coffin and associates built an elaborate chain of "stations" in Indiana, along which they were able to pass fugitives in transit. Thomas Garrett, a Delaware Friend, was said to have aided more than two thousand seven hundred runaways, though a man of family and wealth, with much to lose. He was candid and notorious in his hatred of slavery and his willingness to service all runaways. Yet Garrett was only caught at his work following years of activity. The severe fine imposed on him was said to have ruined him temporarily; friends and admirers helped him reestablish his business in iron products. Notable was Garrett's declaration in court that he did not intend to stint his duties toward fugitive slaves as he saw it.

Numerous others from Delaware to Illinois and all the way to the Canadian border not only studded the North with "underground stations," but acted directly in bringing slaves out of bondage. Thus Calvin Fairbank, an Oberlin College graduate, and long concerned for fugitive slaves, in 1844 went into Kentucky to bring out the wife of a Negro runaway from slavery. Captured, Fairbank served five years of a jail sentence, and, pardoned, returned to his work. He was again seized, this time in Indiana, and returned to prison in Kentucky, not to emerge again until 1864.

Although all Negroes, free or slave, were far from committed to freedom enterprises any more than all whites were, and though northern and southern Negro communities harbored predictable assortments of lightminded elements and "Judases" capable of informing on fugitives and alleged fugitives, there were certainly strong currents among Negroes which gave them power in fugitive slave operations. They harbored fugitives, moved them East, West, and North to friends, raised money for them, and performed many other services of mercy and affection. Alone, however, they could have accomplished only a tithe of the "underground" work which was actually performed. And the effort to publicize and develop this work —to implicate skeptics in it on grounds of humanity, and to bring out the moral meaning of the underground railroad, particularly important because it transgressed the law of the land—could only be done by white orators, clergymen, and others who could not be ignored by their families and associates, their audiences and their congregations. Frederick Douglass was one of the greatest of abolitionist spokesmen, but, alone, he would have had no voice. William Still, a distinguished Philadelphia Negro, who later prepared one of the vital chronicles of northern labors for fugitive slaves, *The Underground Railroad* (1873) never thought to do anything but honor his white coadjutors. His indispensable book (along with Wilbur H. Siebert's masterly *The Underground Railroad from Slavery to Freedom* [1899]) is a monument of tribute to white heroes and heroines as well as to his own people.

Viewpoint 4

"When fugitive slaves did receive aid [from the Underground Railroad] it was mostly by chance and after they had succeeded in completing the most dangerous part of their journey."

The Underground Railroad Was Largely a Myth

Larry Gara

In his book *The Liberty Line: The Legend of the Underground Railroad*, historian Larry Gara maintains that pre–Civil War propaganda and post–Civil War exaggerations have distorted much of the history of the Undergound Railroad. In the following viewpoint adapted from his book, Gara argues that while many antislavery whites and free northern blacks did help slaves escape, the mythology of the Underground Railroad has overshadowed the active role that slaves played in their own escape. Runaway slaves usually made the most difficult part of their escape through the South alone, writes Gara. The aid that northern abolitionists most often provided was in the form of preventing runaways from being captured and returned under the Fugitive Slave Law of 1850.

Of all the legends growing out of the Civil War era and the slavery struggle preceding it, none has taken deeper root in popular thought than that of the underground railroad. Although details are usually indistinct, the term still suggests a widespread, highly secret conspiracy to transport slaves from southern bondage to northern freedom. The railroad operated a very busy line, despite the constant dangers its employees faced. And the abolitionist operators usually outwitted the road's would-be sabateurs with such tricks as secret rooms and passageways, instant disguises, and many other devices based on ingenuity and daring. It was an abolitionist institution and most of its willing passengers would have been helpless without the road's many services.

Exaggeration and Distortion

The underground railroad of legend, like most legendary institutions, is a blend of fiction and fact. Most of the historical source material which provided the basis for the traditional view of the institution was not recorded until long after the events took place, much of it in the post–Civil War era when abolitionists and their descendants wrote their reminiscences or handed down the anecdotes of exciting times by word of mouth. With one major exception, the books published after the Civil War containing firsthand underground railroad accounts view the events from the standpoint of the white abolitionists. As all historical sources reflect the bias of their writers, abolitionist sources tended to view the ante bellum past as a morality play with themselves in the role of righteous crusaders, Southerners as the villains, and the fugitive slaves as helpless, passive recipients of aid. The former antislavery activists were recalling a time of high danger and excitement. When Professor Wilbur H. Siebert contacted hundreds of abolitionists in the 1890's for material for his history of the underground railroad, one wrote him: "There was a peculiar *fascination* about that 'U.G.R.R.' biz., that *fires me up*, even now when I recall the scenes of excitement and danger."

In retrospect, the romance of underground railroad work inevitably led to some exaggeration. There was some organized assistance provided in a few northern communities for fleeing slaves, but there was nothing resembling a nationally organized

effort, and much of the aid was rendered on a temporary and hap-
hazard basis. With the passage of time one or two well-known incidents concerning fugitives and those who helped them sometimes created a popular image of a busy underground line in a
particular locale. Well-known figures in the anti-slavery movement were often associated with underground railroad activity,
whether or not they had actually participated in that phase of the
effort. When Professor Siebert contacted the Reverend Joshua
Young of Groton, Massachusetts, for his experiences, Young
replied that he could tell very little. "Perhaps my connection with
the U.G.R.R. has been exaggerated," he explained, "owing to the
circumstances of my being the only present and officiating cler-
gyman at John Brown's funeral, which gave me some prominence
among abolitionists."

Not all the former abolitionists were as modest as the Reverend
Young; in the postwar period individuals and their relatives sometimes expanded on their actual adventures in underground railroad work. Thus family pride contributed to the legend. Among
other things, those people who had been scorned and ridiculed in
many communities now had their position vindicated. Thrilling
stories were recounted at gatherings of northern local historical
societies, repeated in hundreds of newspapers, and often found
their way into the county histories which were published in the
1880's. Communities as well as individuals claimed an unblem-
ished record of sacrificial service to the victims of slavery who were
fleeing from its toils. Hardly a town in the North was without its
local legends or a house reputed to have been a major depot on
the underground line. Very few such places have had their historical reputations verified, and in some instances even houses
built after the Civil War came to share an underground railroad
reputation.

One of the more serious distortions caused by the legend of the
underground railroad concerns the role of the fugitives themselves. An overemphasis on the amount of assistance rendered by
white abolitionists has tended to make the people the railroad was
designed to aid—the fugitive slaves—either invisible or passive
and helpless without aid from others. In fact, they were anything
but passive. The thousands of slaves who left the South usually

planned and carried out their own escape plans. They were careful, determined, and imaginative in devising such plans.

The Efforts of the Slaves Themselves

Some slaves merely ran off, traveling by night and resting by day, with assistance from other slaves, free black persons, and occasionally sympathetic whites, not necessarily abolitionists. Others made contact with and paid ship captains running from southern to northern ports to hide them among the cargo. When viewed from the perspective of the slave narratives dictated or written by the former slaves themselves, the whole fugitive slave epoch takes on a different emphasis with more attention to the fugitives' own self-help efforts, though credit is accorded abolitionist assistance when it was given.

Often there was no help available, either in planning or carrying out slave escapes, and in light of such circumstances a successful escape was a major accomplishment of the human spirit. In 1838 Charles Ball traveled 1,200 miles from Alabama to New York, unaided by any underground railroad. Ball journeyed at night, living mostly on roots and berries, and contacted abolitionists only after he reached New York. Another slave took an entire year to reach Cincinnati from Alabama. The scant records which are available indicate that many escaping slaves were afraid to trust any outside assistance, preferring to rely as little as possible on others.

Since free blacks were legally obligated to carry certificates of freedom at all times, the fugitives frequently borrowed free papers or had them forged. When Frederick Douglass succeeded in leaving slavery he borrowed the "protection papers" of an American sailor, but it was only in the postwar edition of his autobiography that he revealed his method of escape. Disguise was also commonly used by fugitives. Light-colored slaves sometimes posed as white travelers. When Lewis Clarke left Kentucky slavery, he wore only dark glasses to disguise himself. Clarke stayed in hotels and taverns along the way and reached Ohio safely, later continuing his journey to Canada.

One of the most imaginative and daring of slave escape plans was that devised and carried out by William and Ellen Craft of

Macon, Georgia. Ellen, who was the daughter of her own master and of very light complexion, posed as an elderly and infirm southern gentleman with a bandaged head and one arm in a sling. The Crafts used the sling in order to make it impossible for the traveling "master" to sign necessary forms and to register at hotels, a ploy to hide Ellen's illiteracy. William played the part of a loyal personal servant. He was a skilled cabinetmaker who had earned enough of his own money to purchase a railroad ticket from Georgia to Philadelphia. The Crafts played their roles well. Except for a brief moment of near-disaster in Baltimore when a railroad ticket agent wanted Ellen to sign a form and provide a bond for her servant, the couple had no trouble along the way.

A free black fellow passenger gave the Crafts the name of an abolitionist in Philadelphia; this was their first knowledge of any possible aid from such a source. They rested briefly in Philadelphia before going on to Boston, where they made their home until they fled the country to elude agents of their former owner. The Crafts recorded their remarkable escape story in a pamphlet, "Running a Thousand Miles for Freedom, or the Escape of William and Ellen Craft from Slavery," published in England.

Henry Brown, a slave in Richmond, Virginia, used an equally daring method to escape from slavery. He decided to have himself crated and shipped north by railway express. The plan was Brown's, but of course it required an accomplice. Brown contacted Samuel A. Smith, a sympathetic white man, who followed instructions and, for a fee of $40, sent the crate to the Philadelphia Anti-Slavery Office. Brown's safe arrival was hailed as a miracle in the antislavery press. Later he spoke to numerous abolitionist gatherings, exhibiting the box used in his flight from slavery, along with a powerful diorama showing many scenes of southern slave life, painted for him by Benjamin Roberts, a black artist from Boston. Meanwhile, Samuel Smith helped several others to escape and was apprehended and convicted for his efforts, serving eight years in a Virginia prison. Henry "Box" Brown and the Crafts were frequently referred to as "passengers" on the underground railroad, even though their escapes were planned and largely carried out by themselves, certainly not according to the usual transportation service that institution brings to mind.

The Efforts of Individual Abolitionists

When fugitive slaves did receive aid it was mostly by chance and after they had succeeded in completing the most dangerous part of their journey through the southern states. There were abolitionists who made the underground railroad a kind of special concern though the aid they provided was on a regional rather than a national basis. Two who were very active in this phase of the antislavery work were Levi Coffin and Thomas Garrett, both Quakers. Coffin lived and worked in Newport, Indiana, for more than twenty years, then moved to Cincinnati, where he added a degree of local organization to the efforts of those who were already helping runaway slaves. Coffin and his friends transported fugitives in wagons from one town to another, on occasion having to elude slave hunters. They also provided the former slaves with clothing and other necessities, and sometimes boarded them until they could be transported or sent by themselves farther north. Much of Levi Coffin's underground railroad work was aboveboard, especially as antislavery sentiment strengthened in the years just preceding the Civil War. He recorded in his memoirs, written many years later, that public opinion in his neighborhood became so strongly antislavery that he kept fugitives at his house "openly, while preparing them for their journey to the North."

Thomas Garrett provided skillful leadership in assisting fugitive slaves in and around Wilmington, Delaware, working closely with others in Chester County, Pennsylvania, and the Philadelphia area. Garrett spared neither time nor expense in his efforts, which usually involved sheltering fugitives, making arrangements for their transportation, and paying necessary expenses. Several times he assisted Harriet Tubman, who, having escaped herself, made trips into the South to rescue others. Although Delaware was a slave state, Garrett capitalized on its unusual degree of free speech and freedom of the press and he seldom worked in secrecy. Sued for damages by a number of slave owners who won verdicts against him totalling nearly $8,000, Garrett eventually settled for a quarter of that amount, still a considerable sum of money.

Thomas Garrett, Levi Coffin, and other abolitionists involved in the work of assisting fugitive slaves nearly always concentrated their efforts in their own localities. With very few exceptions, such locally organized assistance was unavailable in the South, and even the more militant abolitionists declined to entice slaves from their bondage. Levi Coffin made frequent business trips into the South, but never had any trouble while there. Although he spoke openly of his opposition to slavery, he assured his southern acquaintances that it was not his business while in the South "to interfere with their laws or their slaves." Others believed the risk outweighed the benefits. James H. Fairchild, president of Oberlin College, recalled that the majority of Oberlin abolitionists did not consider it "legitimate to go into the Slave States and entice the slaves from their masters." While they denied the master's ownership they looked upon venturing into the South as a "reckless undertaking, involving too much risk, and probably doing more harm than good." It is no wonder then that the former slaves who recorded their escape accounts tell of plans and daring journeys involving only themselves.

All of the prosecutions under the Federal Fugitive Slave Act of 1850 were for acts allegedly committed in the North. Although only about a dozen cases were prosecuted, they received a great deal of public attention and did much to popularize antislavery and anti-southern sentiment. The act itself met with widespread criticism and opposition in the northern states. As part of the Compromise of 1850 it was designed to mollify the slave interests, but its blatant violation of the rights of anyone accused of being a fugitive slave gave a powerful propaganda weapon to the antislavery forces. They pointed out that there was no provision for a jury trial for alleged fugitives and that in fact the law, which they usually referred to as a "bill," denied the protection of free soil to fleeing slaves and made slavery a national rather than a sectional institution. Many Northerners who had little concern for the slaves themselves resented this intrusion of the slave power into their free society.

When fugitives were captured and returned to slavery the effect on northern public opinion was even stronger. Anthony Burns, a former Virginia slave living in Boston, was arrested on May 24, 1854, only days after the Senate passed the unpopular Kansas-Nebraska Bill opening new territories to slave expansion. A group of people, most of them black, tried to break into the courthouse where Burns was held and rescue him. In the scuffle one officer was killed and later there were arrests for that act, but no conviction. With extraordinary security the Government was able to try Burns and order his return to slavery.

The day Anthony Burns left Boston the church bells tolled and the line of march was draped in mourning crepe. Thousands of disgusted citizens watched while contingents of police, twenty-two companies of Massachusetts soldiers, and a battery of artillery guarded the fugitive. One scholar estimated that Burns's rendition cost $100,000, yet the nationally publicized event converted many to the antislavery point of view. One abolitionist urged William Lloyd Garrison to publish the entire Burns history, believing that "it furnishes far more important materials for History, than it would have furnished had the man been rescued."

Much of the publicity concerning Anthony Burns was promoted by the Boston Vigilance Committee, one of several such committees founded or reactivated in response to the Fugitive Slave Law of 1850. The work of these committees contributed substantially to the popular image of the underground railroad, though much of their work was aboveboard and routine. Some were founded by Negroes and all of them used black sympathizers as contacts and workers. One of the more active was the Philadelphia Vigilance Committee with William Still, a black abolitionist, as chairman. Approximately 100 fugitives a year received assistance from the committee during the eight-year period when William Still kept records of its work. Still and committee members also interviewed each of the former slaves, carefully recorded essential facts, and preserved the organization's financial records and some of its correspondence. William Still later used this and other first-hand material in compiling his important book, *The Underground Rail Road*. As a Negro he was concerned that the fugitives receive credit as well as those whites who risked much to help them. Still wrote, promoted, and sold his book through agents. He hoped the work would inspire other blacks to greater efforts until they could gain wealth and produce literary works of quality. As the only book-length account of the underground railroad written by a black author, Still's volume is unique.

In the years before the Civil War the underground railroad also provided a wealth of propaganda material for the antislavery cause. Incidents concerning fugitives and their rescue, often by black crowds, were frequently reported in the reform press. Abolitionists boasted of their underground railroad activity and published details of escapes to arouse further sympathy for the fugitives and the antislavery cause. Sometimes escaped slaves were exhibited at abolitionist meetings. Available assistance was even listed in some of the antislavery newspapers along with the narratives of former slaves. Nearly every aspect of the activity had potential for winning new free soil or antislavery converts. The fugitives aroused sympathy, for their treatment by southern slave hunters and by the courts violated all sense of decency and respect for civil liberties. All of this contributed to a growing resentment of the encroachments and demands of what Northerners referred to as the slave power.

It was in the years after the Civil War had destroyed the slave power and its hold on the nation that the underground railroad assumed the character of a cherished American legend. Many Northerners viewed the past and the defeated slave interests with a vision distorted by the course of events. The immorality of slavery became obvious with its defeat, and some who had had only marginal connections with free soil or antislavery efforts were prone to exaggerate their contributions. As early as 1864 abolitionist Lydia Maria Child remarked to William Lloyd Garrison that new antislavery friends were "becoming as plenty as roses in June," and she marveled "at their power of keeping a secret so long!" A year later an abolitionist reported that it was "rare to meet one who has ever wished well to slavery, or desired anything but its final abolition."

A Complex Historical Picture

The romantic nature of underground railroad activity virtually assured its place in Civil War tradition. In the 1890's, when Professor Siebert corresponded with hundreds of abolitionists and their descendants, only a few denied having valid recollections of the institution. Journalists and local historians in many northern communities took for granted an underground railroad record, and to some Northerners the thousands of slaves who escaped became millions.

A pattern of action emerged in these accounts, with emphasis on the role of white abolitionists, a pattern which was repeated in a number of works of fiction as well as in some historical writing. Consequently, the black participants became virtually invisible in the underground railroad of legend. Exposing the distortions and oversimplifications associated with the underground railroad in the years since the Civil War should not denigrate those abolitionists who were actively involved, nor should it minimize the importance of their efforts. The historical picture, however, is much more complex and vastly different from the legendary accounts with their heroes and villains participating in a noble crusade to free helpless victims of slavery. Underground railroad operators did aid some slaves in their escape, but such aid must not overshadow or obliterate the efforts of the slaves to free themselves.

Viewpoint 5

"Of the numerous slave revolts, at least six reached serious stages and had appalling repercussions."

Black Resistance to American Slavery Was Widespread

William F. Cheek

In this excerpt from historian William F. Cheek's 1970 book *Black Resistance Before the Civil War*, the author provides an overview of the various ways in which many slaves resisted bondage and forced labor. According to Cheek, resistance took many forms, which included laboring halfheartedly, running away, committing acts of individual violence, and organizing outright rebellions. He provides numerous anecdotes of such resistance and also details the circumstances surrounding some of the most serious slave revolts in American history, including those led by Denmark Vesey in 1822 and Nat Turner in 1831. Cheek concludes that slaves' record of resistance is a proud one.

M any thousands of slaves chose to fight the system that bound them by running away, so many, in fact, that a regular feature of practically every issue of every Southern newspaper was the listing of runaway slave advertisements. However, only a small fraction of those who made the attempt were able to reach an area where they could be free. Although estimates of the number of fugitive slaves range as high as sixty thousand to one hundred thousand, the most recently published student of the problem, Larry Gara, who wisely does not commit himself to a specific estimate, believes the figure was substantially lower. One thing is certain, however: in the face of overwhelming odds, black men and women, sometimes with their children, persistently tried to escape.

Runaways Were Common

How to keep "De Old Folks at Home" was perhaps the most time consuming and expensive of all the slaveholder's difficulties in managing his estate. Reluctant to acknowledge any imperfections in the system of slavery or in their own administration of it, many masters (sometimes with justification) blamed outsiders—abolitionists and free Negroes—for putting the idea of freedom in the minds of the slaves. Samuel Cartwright, a doctor of medicine at the University of Louisiana, came up with another diagnosis: runaways, he wrote quite seriously, suffered from "Draptomania, or the Disease Causing Negroes to Run Away."

Those who attempted escape were predominately, but by no means exclusively, the young, the energetic, the independent, and the intelligent. (Advertisements often described runaways as "talented and wily," "very intelligent," "uncommonly bright.") Flight, for at least some of the young, may have been stimulated by the identity crisis that, to a degree, affects all youth. For these slaves, running away represented a crucial rejection of "parental" authority, in their case the authority of the master. Vulnerable at once to hurt and hope, anxious to throw off the old and get on with the new, seeking to pledge their energies to a daring undertaking, these young slaves, it seems reasonable to suggest, were establishing their manhood as they made their break for freedom.

For all runaways, the principal motivation was the desire to be free, but any number of factors could trigger the flight. Consistent overwork and poor treatment, or perhaps a sudden change in conditions, such as impending sale or punishment, might be the catalytic circumstance. After a slave had committed a crime, or been charged with committing one, it was to be expected that he would try to escape. The family situation was a further consideration: the slave might leave to join a loved one or to get away from an unloved one; or he might run away in retaliation for the splitting up of his family by the owner. Then too, news that one more slave had gotten free or a camp meeting's rousing exhortation to freedom might embolden yet another to escape.

But there was much to deter potential fugitives. Strict surveillance, compounded with paternalism, weakened their resolve. Furthermore, the ignorant, superstitious, and fearful, naturally enough, preferred the devil they knew to the devil they might find outside. With scant experience of the world beyond the immediate plantation environs, most were in the position of the ex-slave who admitted he "had heard tell of a free country—but I did not know where it was, nor how to get there." Moreover, if flight were attempted, food and security would be difficult to find, and if flight were to fail, slaves well knew, punishment or sale into the deeper South almost certainly awaited. The pain of parting from family and friends restrained others. "It is my opinion," Frederick Douglass remarked, "that thousands would escape from slavery who now remain, but for the strong cords of affection that bind them to their friends."

Yet they did run away and, if caught, sometimes ran away again and even again. Possibly affecting disguises and traveling usually at night, the fugitives, who left singly or in an occasional group of as many as fifty, headed in all directions away from the plantation. The fortunate ones escaped to Canada, to Mexico, to Spanish Louisiana, and to Florida. (In Florida they allied with the Seminoles and fought two wars, the first in 1812–1818 and the second in 1835–1842, against the United States.) During the American Revolution and the War of 1812, thousands fled behind British lines. . . .

The commitment to run away had a hard finality about it. As one slave explained, "if they undertake to escape, it is with a feeling of victory or death—they determine not to be taken alive, if possible to prevent it even by bloodshed." There were stories about slaves like Margaret Garner who, when she discovered the Negro catchers hot on her heels, tried to kill all her children and did succeed in stabbing one to death.

The philosophy undergirding the commitment was perhaps most succinctly expressed by William Wells Brown who, in his slave narrative, observed: "If I wish to stand up and say, 'I am a man,' I must leave the land that gave me birth."

Resisting Forced Labor

One of the most subtle forms of retaliation against the master was the affecting of the role of Sambo, or Uncle Tom. Ironically enough it was the slaveowner himself who, to some degree, invented the role. Slaves, he averred many times, were naturally lazy, irresponsible, fawning, childlike, docile, and helpless. For if white Southerners could convince themselves and others that blacks were really inferior, they could justify maintaining slavery. But Sambo was far more the creation of the black Southerner. Moreover, it was a deliberate creation, even though, as Stanley Elkins, in a brilliantly controlled statement (*Slavery*), has pointed out, the absolute power of the Southern enslaver over the enslaved doubtless did cause some slaves to become permanently infantilized. An impressive body of social-psychological research reveals that some persons, slaves or no, can play a role with such intensity that, over a period of time, the role and the personality become indistinguishable. Most slaves, however, willfully fell to playing the Sambo role for reasons of survival and resistance. "The only weapon of self-defense that I could use successfully," noted ex-slave Henry Bibb, "was that of deception." Behind the mask, the slave could hide a simple desire to get out of work or gain a reward, along with his enjoyment at the luxury of having put something over on the master. Or Sambo could be masking an emotion so complex he did not really comprehend it: for example, his need to ease guilt feelings over his abiding hatred of his master.

Stupidity, incompetence, slowness were all components of the disguise. Douglass commented that "slaveholders ever underrate the intelligence with which they have to grapple," noting that among his co-laborers, a popular proverb was: "Where ignorance is bliss, 'tis folly to be wise." Was it ignorance or deception when slave mothers fell asleep over their sick children, thus forcing the white mistress to remain up through the night to care for them?

Was it ignorance or deception when slaves refused to take up a trade? Was it ignorance or deception when blacks worked so poorly that numbers of whites had to be present to direct and help them? . . .

Slaves slogged through their work days half-heartedly; consequently, their labor yielded less than could have been produced by free men. By insisting that certain tasks demanded more than one worker, slaves aided one another in reducing the work load. A naive Southern diarist, Susan Smedes, wrote despairingly that an entire afternoon was used up by two of the men to butcher a sheep. Sometimes blacks performed so inadequately that one of the white men on the plantation was forced, disgustedly, to finish off the work himself. . . .

Feigning illness was another method of resistance, one that an owner had especial difficulty in handling. Often he found it better to accept the slave's word than to accuse him of sham, and send him back to the fields, only to have him turn out to be really sick. [Historian Frederick] Olmsted cited one such case, when a slave had died, the owner lamenting: "He was a good eight hundred dollar nigger, and it was a lesson to me about taming possums, that I ain't going to forget in a hurry." On the auction block, a slave might pretend to be sick so that he would not be sold or would bring a smaller price, in order to spite the master, or perhaps, so that his new owner might give him a lighter work load. Feigned pregnancies were not uncommon even though, at the end of nine months, punishment was certain. According to Susan Smedes, one slave faked blindness for years and was given few duties, but after being freed was able to harvest some eighteen crops. It is worthwhile to note that, in the few compilations of plantation records of slave sicknesses made to date, the sick rolls were the longest at those times of the year when the work load was heaviest. Furthermore, there was a high incidence of ailments on Saturday work days, and very few on Sunday rest days.

Individual Acts of Violence

The agony of slavery pushed some black men and women to resist through desperate acts of self-violence. To avoid work or auction block, slaves chopped off fingers and toes. They plied themselves with herbs that induced vomiting and with drugs that induced miscarriage. Dirt-eating rendered others unfit for work and, eventually, killed them. In *The Peculiar Institution*, Kenneth Stampp cites such instances as that of the Arkansas slave who, whenever wearied by work, would throw his left shoulder out of place, and of another man who was kicked by a mule and continued to aggravate the bruise whenever it began to heal. The desperation extended to suicide and a peculiar form of mercy killing. Ex-slave accounts tell of the woman who hurled herself out a window to escape the rape-minded slave catcher, and of the runaway who slit his throat on board the ship that was carrying him back to slavery, and of Elizabeth, who smothered her own child.

Slave resistance was manifested in other types of violence or crime—and as Jordan has asked how do you distinguish crime from resistance among slaves?—including theft, arson, maiming, as well as poisoning and other forms of murder. Petty thievery was common, taking in such necessaries as money, clothing, food and animals, as well as such comforts as whiskey, wine, and jewelry. After theft, the most pervasive crime was arson. Seeking revenge for a general or specific wrong, slaves fired homes of overseers and masters, farm buildings, cotton gins, and fields. In the 1790's some citizens of Charleston were sufficiently alarmed to try to persuade others to build with brick and stone rather than wood. So widespread was arson that for a time the American Fire Insurance Company refused to insure any property in the South.

Provoked to sudden rage or brooding over accumulated injustices, slaves were driven to strike out at the white man over them, sometimes to kill him. How badly the white man was injured might depend on what weapon was available to the slave, stick or rock, brick or hoe, rope or knife, hatchet or axe. One ex-slave revealed that on his plantation blacks were given to stringing a rope across the road to knock passing riders from their horses; and another told of an old slave who, having been bullwhipped by the overseer, struck him in the head with a stick and then took up an axe, and chopped off his hands and feet. Into the master's food or drink house servants covertly slipped such poisons as arsenic, laudanum, ratsbane, and the seed of the jimson weed. It was a form of revenge peculiarly suited to women. After hearing that her master had provided for her in his will in the event he left no heirs, one slave woman proceeded to poison his three children, one by one. Actually, not a few slaves did murder the overseer or master or mistress or even, occasionally, the whole family. In Virginia alone, records reveal that between 1786 and 1810 thirty-one slaves were executed for killing masters and overseers. . . .

Organized Revolts and Rebellions

Beyond day-by-day resistance, revolts erupted from time to time during the entire span of slavery, occurring as early as 1663 in Gloucester County, Virginia, and breaking out periodically thereafter in rural and urban areas of both North and South. Some were elaborately planned and organized and had as their intention the destruction of the slave system and the creation of a black state; others tended to be more haphazardly put together and aimed only at wiping out the slaveholder's life and property. Still

"A Troublesome Property"

Kenneth M. Stampp, in his 1956 book The Peculiar Institution, *was one of the first historians to write extensively about slave resistance and refute the old stereotype of the submissive and contented slave. He was also one of the first historians to include passive resistance, and not just open insurrection, in his coverage of the subject.*

If slaves yielded to authority most of the time, they did so because they usually saw no other practical choice. Yet few went through life without expressing discontent somehow, some time. Even the most passive slaves, usually before they reached middle age, flared up in protest now and then. The majority, as they grew older, lost hope and spirit. Some, however, never quite gave in, never stopped fighting back in one way or another. The "bad character" of this "insolent," "surly," and "unruly" sort made them a liability to those who owned them, for a slave's value was measured by his disposi-

others were concerned mainly with throwing off the bonds of servitude through flight. . . .

Underlying all the other causes for revolt was the massive injustice that emanated from, indeed, was at the very core of the South's peculiar social system. As Hannah Arendt, and before her Herman Melville in *Billy Budd*, has pointed out, there are those fearful times when violence appears to be the only possibility for righting an awful wrong. This is not to say it is right. It is rather to note with sadness what one can expect from human beings when they are treated brutally by other human beings.

Of the numerous slave revolts, at least six reached serious stages and had appalling repercussions. In 1712 in New York City more than two dozen slaves fired a building and killed at least nine men, wounding several others. The city, chilled by the murders of a Long Island family only four years earlier, for which four slaves had been executed, reacted quickly and without mercy. Soldiers

tion as much as by his strength and skills. Such rebels seldom won legal freedom, yet they never quite admitted they were slaves.

Slave resistance, whether bold and persistent or mild and sporadic, created for all slaveholders a serious problem of discipline. As authors or as readers they saw the problem discussed in numberless essays with such titles as "The Management of Negroes," essays which filled the pages of southern agricultural periodicals. Many masters had reason to agree with the owner of a hundred slaves who complained that he possessed "just 100 troubles," or with the North Carolina planter who said that slaves were "a troublesome property."

The record of slave resistance forms a chapter in the story of the endless struggle to give dignity to human life. Though the history of southern bondage reveals that men *can* be enslaved under certain conditions, it also demonstrates that their love of freedom is hard to crush.

Kenneth M. Stampp, *The Peculiar Institution*. New York: Knopf, 1956.

from a nearby fort rounded up most of the rebels in a matter of hours, although several evaded capture by taking their own lives. The remainder were executed: thirteen were hanged, one was suspended in chains in the town until death, three were burned, one being roasted over a slow fire, and one was broken on the wheel. Twenty-nine years later, against a backdrop of severe winter and economic suffering, with the added aggravation of several barn-burnings by Negroes across the river in Hackensack and the threat of a Spanish invasion, New York City again was enveloped in tragedy. A series of fires broke out at key governmental buildings, and the rumor spread quickly that Negroes had been seen in the area. Whether an actual slave conspiracy existed can never be known; but, in any event, the facts made little difference to a community engulfed in hysteria. Well over a hundred and fifty persons, including some whites who were thought to be accomplices, were rounded up; thirty-one slaves were finally executed, another seventy were driven out of the colony.

The most serious revolt of the colonial period, in which more than twenty white persons were killed, erupted in Stono, South Carolina, southwest of Charleston, in 1739. Previous months had seen hard economic conditions, slave guerrilla warfare, and rumors of a conspiracy which had led to the arrest of three slaves. In addition, South Carolina's population was heavily imbalanced, black over white. One September day a group of slaves met at Stono, where they killed the guards at a warehouse and stocked up on arms and ammunition, and then marched out into the countryside "with colours flying and drums beating." Heading to the southwest, toward Spanish territory where they could find refuge, they killed the whites and burned the plantations on their route, picking up more slaves as they went, until their number reached an estimated fifty to one hundred. When they stopped to rest and celebrate, the militia caught up with them and surrounded the field, and, in the encounter that followed a number were killed. In the next months, others were captured and put to death.

In the hot late summer of 1800, a young giant of a man named Gabriel Prosser, but called "General" by his fellow slaves, conspired to gain control of Richmond, and perhaps the whole state of Virginia, to set up a black commonwealth. Reputed to possess an "intellect above his rank in life," Gabriel derived his inspiration from "divine signals" and an exposure to the French revolutionary philosophy. For some weeks before the target date, he matured his plans, organizing a cadre, pinpointing strategic installations in the city, and accumulating a small cache of weapons. During the same period he enlisted an indeterminate but decidedly substantial number of recruits, later reckoned by frightened witnesses at from two thousand to fifty thousand. On the appointed day, Gabriel and his men gathered outside the city. But nature—the impartial nature of the weather, which rains on the powerful and the rebellious alike, and the capricious nature of man, with his tragically divided loyalties—aborted the insurrection. A storm, bringing "enormous rain," hindered the movements of Gabriel's forces, washing out a key bridge and making normally quiet streams impassable, even as two slaves were informing on their fellows. Retaliation ensued, so bloody that Thomas Jefferson was provoked to remark, "We are truly to be pitied."

Denmark Vesey and Nat Turner

In the same year Gabriel lost his bid to escape slavery, Denmark Vesey won a $1,500 lottery and purchased his freedom. Prior to his good fortune, Vesey had been the long-time personal servant of Captain Joseph Vesey, a slave trader, and so had travelled widely, gaining facility in several languages. Once freed, Vesey set up a carpentry shop in Charleston, South Carolina. Over the next years he acquired money and property, and built a reputation for industry and integrity among both whites and blacks. Living free, however, he had a vantage point from which to evaluate the debasement of all black men, regardless of their legal status, as well as an unusual opportunity to take independent action. He began to jibe at the slaves and free Negroes who hung around his shop over their passivity and subservience to the white man. Moreover, he joined the African Methodist Episcopal Church, later becoming a preacher, where he argued that God's intention was for black people to be free. Stressing the parallels between the children of Israel and the slaves of the South, Vesey told his congregations of the work of the abolitionists. . . .

Around Christmas of 1821, when he felt his arguments had

been properly received and disseminated, Vesey began to build a secret organization geared to rebellion. In the next months he showed himself to be both a dedicated revolutionary and a skilled psychologist. Only the most intelligent and capable slaves, along with the leaders of the A.M.E. church, were enlisted, and they were warned that once a commitment had been made, they could not retreat. Furthermore, his closest lieutenants were selected for their peculiar qualities and positions, granted them because of their owners' trust. Rolla, servant of the governor of South Carolina, a position with obvious advantages for the plotters, was described as "bold" and "ardent," with "uncommon self-possession." The ship carpenter Peter Poyas, as foresighted as he was determined, has been quoted as warning: "Don't mention it to those waiting-men who receive presents of old coats from their masters, or they'll betray us." Gullah Jack, master of witchcraft, was brought in to give his supernatural blessing to the conspirators, some of whom were true believers. Along the line of occult persuasion, Vesey himself might well have played up his own epilepsy to sway the superstitious.

Only the small group of leaders was aware of the plan that called for a six-pronged attack on Charleston on Sunday, July 16, 1822. Orders were to seize all arms and ammunition and to cut down all whites. Further, Vesey informed his followers that help could probably be expected from the Haitians, whom he had written, and that their ships might await at the docks to take the rebels to Haiti. As an added stimulus to revolt, the conspirators spread rumors that whites intended to massacre blacks on the Fourth of July. In fact, something like that did happen. It was too optimistic to expect that Vesey's terrible secret could be kept for so long. In late May an unauthorized recruiter attempted to sign up a "faithful" house slave. Ultimately forty-two men were banished, thirty-five executed.

Again in 1800, the year when Gabriel died and Denmark Vesey bought his way out of slavery, Nat Turner was born in Southampton County, Virginia. His African mother, it is reported, was so upset at giving birth to a child who would be a slave that she had to be restrained from killing him. As is the case for most slave revolutionaries, little is known of Nat's life, but from the rather skimpy record it appears that he was an exceptional slave. His family life seems to have been notably strong; according to his own testimony, he was taught by his parents to read and write. At one time in his life he ran away, only to return later because he believed he had been divinely instructed to do so. Through years of Bible reading and intermittent visions, Nat became convinced that God intended him "for some great purpose." His mysticism not only provided inspiration but also attracted followers. "Having soon discovered that to be great I must appear so," he explained, "I studiously avoided mixing in society and wrapped myself in mystery, devoting my time to fasting and prayer."

On August 21, 1831, after he had fully prepared himself, and having read the proper signs in the heavens, Nat called his followers together to map final plans. That night he and five other slaves set out, armed with axes and clubs, gathering forces as they moved from plantation to plantation. Turner later declared, "indiscriminate slaughter was not their intention after they obtained a foothold, and was resorted to in the first instance to strike terror and alarm. Women and children would afterwards have been spared, and men too who ceased to resist." Whatever his intention, some fifty-five white persons were killed before a combined force of the army, the militia, and numerous white volunteers— some three thousand men in all—could put down the rebellion. The white forces did not stop with Turner's band, but went on to slaughter blacks at random throughout the area; the dead finally numbered nearly two hundred.

Harriet Jacobs, an ex-Virginia slave, later reflected sardonically: "Not far from this time Nat Turner's insurrection broke out; and the news threw our town into great commotion. Strange that they should be alarmed, when their slaves were so contented and happy."

Viewpoint 6

"The realities of power and geography in the Old South . . . minimized the kind of slave rebellion that often occurred in the other New World plantation societies."

Open Rebellion Against American Slavery Was Relatively Limited

John B. Boles

Historians generally recognize only a handful of major slave revolts in the American South, and the most notorious of those— Gabriel Prosser's Insurrection of 1800, Denmark Vesey's conspiracy of 1822, and Nat Turner's Rebellion of 1831—all failed. In contrast, Brazil witnessed an estimated twenty-five slave revolts in the nineteenth century, which culminated in the abolition of slavery in Brazil in 1888. There were also slave revolts in other areas of Latin American and the Caribbean that were more violent and more successful than those in the United States.

In the following viewpoint historian John B. Boles of Rice University argues that geography and the culture of plantation society in the Old South combined to make slave rebellions in

John B. Boles, *Black Southerners, 1619–1869*. Lexington: The University of Kentucky Press, 1983. Copyright © 1983 by The University of Kentucky Press. Reproduced by permission.

the region both rare and very unlikely to succeed. While these factors mitigated against organized rebellion, Boles contends that many individual slaves passively resisted slavery and many others committed individual acts of rebellion.

The one overriding fact about slave rebellion in the Old South was the almost complete absence of large-scale armed insurrection such as occurred in Latin America and the Caribbean and lay like a horrible specter in the back of the minds of countless southern planters. Explaining nonoccurrences is always difficult, and this case is no exception. But even a partial explanation does shed light on two important components of any historical analysis, the comparative and the temporal. The situation in the South after about 1800 was significantly different from that elsewhere in the Americas. Moreover, one must remember the wide variety of rebellious acts that stopped short of insurrection, rebellious acts as diverse and individualized as the planter-slave confrontations themselves. Yet during the heyday of the Old South, in the final decades before the Civil War when cotton was king and the slave population was at its highest, the broad surface of the plantation society was remarkably smooth and stable despite the many small eddies of unrest and the strong, deep current of slaves' cultural and psychological rejection of enslavement. That apparent calm, experienced even by those acute observers who suspected the swirling torrents underneath, has helped perpetuate many myths about the Old South and its two peoples, black and white.

Geography and Population Density

Many factors mitigated against successful armed insurrection by slaves in the Old South. Unlike the situation in Latin America, in the Old South as a whole whites far outnumbered slaves, and of course totally controlled the police power of the states. . . . In certain regions like the sea islands of South Carolina and Georgia and the sugar districts of Louisiana, blacks were in a significant majority, yet even there the distance between individual plantations and the maze of unbridged estuaries, rivers, bayous, sloughs, and swamps made communication and travel between plantations difficult. The geography of the Old South conspired with demography to complicate still further slave attempts at rebellion and escape. Slaves in Brazil and in the Guiana region of northeastern South America, for example, had the huge, unexplored jungle fastness of the Amazon River basin in which to escape; similarly, plantations were located on the perimeters of the West Indian islands, whose interiors offered sure havens for runaways. In both regions slaves escaped to the interior and in maroon [fugitive] settlements often managed to survive for years, occasionally fighting white authorities to a standstill and achieving treaty recognition of their status (often in exchange for returning newly escaped slaves).

This kind of escape from slavery was never possible for the overwhelming majority of bondsmen in the Old South. Except for those few who lived near the Dismal Swamp on the eastern Virginia–North Carolina boundary, and some in Florida and Georgia near the Okefenokee Swamp and the trackless Everglades, there was no safe hinterland where maroons could survive. Moreover, cold winters, particularly in the Upper South, made the prospect of hiding out in the woods uninviting. In the early decades of plantation development, the Indians in the backcountry quickly learned they would be rewarded for capturing and returning slave runaways. The Indians were replaced in later decades by yeoman farmers who either returned the runaways for the reward or kept them. For most slaves the freedom territory north of the Mason-Dixon line or the Ohio River was simply too far away, and while several thousand bondsmen in the last half-century of slavery did escape by way of the Underground Railroad, most of them came from the border states of Maryland and Kentucky.

In Latin America and the Caribbean Islands, where hundreds of slaves lived on huge plantations, the owners were absent, and the working conditions were far more harsh than those typical in the South, desperate slaves, often plagued with famine as well as overwork, occasionally struck out against their brutal oppression and escaped to preexisting maroon communities. The working conditions on the tropical sugar plantations drove slaves to rebellion, and the example of successful escape offered by the maroon settlements in the backcountry emboldened otherwise hesitant bondsmen to act. There was, in other words, a heritage of insurrection in the Caribbean and Latin America that offered slaves not only incentive to rebel but the expectation of success. No such vital spark of hope was possible in the Old South. The few insurrections were small, localized, and quickly and brutally suppressed, with many innocent slaves usually punished and the general restrictions against all slaves made temporarily more harsh.

Family Structures Among Slaves

After 1808 the foreign slave trade to the United States ended, but in the slave societies to the south the transatlantic trade in humans continued. As always, the African imports were disproportionately young males, maintaining the highly unequal slave sex ratios in Latin America and the Caribbean. This, combined with the rigorous work routines, the cruelty of managers on absentee plantations, and the disease-induced high death rates produced a degree of despair that seldom obtained in the Old South. A work force of mostly young males, with neither wives nor families to be concerned about, with expectations of a life that could only be "nasty, brutal, and short," with an almost impenetrable backcountry beckoning them and the ever-present example of successful maroons suggesting that escape was possible, and with the number of superintending whites tiny in proportion to the black population—there is no wonder that out of this unstable situation slave resistance and insurrection were constant realities. Yet by the time there were significant numbers of blacks in the antebellum South, the demographic situation was so different as to provide in effect a check on potential slave unrest.

During the era of the cotton kingdom most slaves were American born, the sex ratio was practically equal (more so than the white ratio), and slaves typically lived in family groupings. As a result the slave family became the single most important bond holding members together, and . . . naming practices and kinship systems evolved to cement relationships made fragile by the possibility of sale or removal. This demographic development also prevented slave insurrection.

Family Bonds Deter Escape

While a population composed mostly of unattached young males can be very explosive (especially when faced with harsh conditions and the possibility of escape), a population where males and females are equally present, family relationships have been formed and there are small children to love and care for, is far more conservative. The possibility of an entire family escaping was practically nil, and parents were loath to forsake their children to save themselves. Likewise few men would leave their loved ones for an escape attempt with little chance of success. If family attachments lessened runaway efforts, so much more did the ties of family affection reduce the possibilities of insurrection. Few male slaves would risk almost sure death when to do so would leave their families fatherless. Moreover, the knowledge that family members and innocent bystanders would be pitilessly punished and their rights severely circumscribed in the aftermath of a rebellion attempt must have restrained many discontented slaves.

In the Old South, where family structures, leisure time, and fairly good living conditions prevented most slaves from being driven into utter desperation, slaves usually found less risky avenues of countering the dehumanization of chattel bondage. Because hunger and abject hopelessness were less common in the Old South, slaves calculated their options more carefully, waiting—sometimes all their lives—for good chances for successful rebellion. Thousands did not find the right moment to strike until the Civil War and the presence of Union troops profoundly changed the balance. Then no one was more shocked than complacent planters when droves of their seemingly most devoted, most responsible slaves "deserted" and chose freedom.

Passive Resistance

The realities of power and geography in the Old South also minimized the kind of slave rebellion that often occurred in the other New World plantation societies. In the antebellum South, slaves were very seldom driven to mindless, suicidal acts of outrage and rebellion. Fully aware of their situation, they learned, socialized, and passed on to their children a wide range of behavior—voice intonations, facial expressions, feigned illness, purposeful laziness and slowness of motion, dumb-like-a-fox incomprehension—that combined equal portions of insubordination and minor rebellion to produce a constant undercurrent of resistance to psychological bondage. Although never completely giving in to authority, most slaves were able, at least in the eyes of their master, to acquiesce in their state of servitude and thus survive with their essential humanity intact. In the most fundamental sense, racial slavery as it existed in the Old South was premised on the assumption by whites that blacks were inferior, either a subhuman or a permanently childlike race. Planters' everyday experience, of course, gave the lie to this assumption, and therein may have been the cause of the guilt that some historians believe troubled many whites, particularly those who constructed elaborate proslavery defenses. Had slaves in general accepted this racial subordination and aspired to be only what the white man prescribed, then blacks would have been total slaves, and all resistance—except occasional outbursts of violence—would have disappeared. But the rich panoply of Afro-American culture, their tales, music, art, and religion protected bondsmen from complete capitulation. Out of the inner reserves of their humanity slaves in measured ways resisted servitude and defended the limited rights that had become, through mutual accommodation, accepted by whites. The black community evolved a culture from which proceeded all forms of slave resistance other than rebellion.

Owners were most concerned with their slaves' labor output, and for that reason bondsmen developed a repertoire of techniques to gain a modicum of control over the amount of work required of them. While some slaves were downright lazy, a low-incentive labor system like slavery obviously gave them few reasons to overexert themselves. Even the application of force soon became counterproductive. Slaves realized they had to work at a moderate pace, for their physical well-being and the stability of their family relationships depended on the success of the plantation. While there was never enough incentive or mobility to turn bondsmen into competitive men-on-the-make, they did accept a responsibility to work at a productivity level that eventually came to be accepted by master and slave alike. Often there was a perpetual low-grade war of wills between the two, with masters cajoling, threatening, and occasionally whipping and slaves complaining, moving at a deliberate pace (though the nature of the crop culture required careful labor that outside observers apparently misunderstood at times for indolence), and even practicing minor agricultural sabotage like breaking tools, "accidentally" plowing up crops, "carelessly" letting the teams get out of the barn-lot, and so on. To what extent owners realized what was going on is problematical; usually they ascribed such behavior to the accepted irresponsibility and childishness of slaves, but surely they at times must have comprehended the guerrilla resistance under way. (It should be said that such sabotage had a negligible effect on the total agricultural system.) Slaves frequently acted dumb, carefully "misunderstood," and—in earlier days—confessed ignorance of English as effective ways to minimize the demands placed on them.

When a master or overseer tried to force slaves to work harder, or longer hours, than convention had come to establish as the norm, slaves were quick to protest. Not only did the war of the wills heat up, but slaves were sometimes quite bold in their insistence against being pushed beyond endurance or general practice. Particularly if an overseer was the offending taskmaster, slaves did not hesitate to take their case to their masters. Whether the overseer was the culprit or not, aggrieved and protesting slaves complained and shuffled along, slowed their pace, and feigned illness. On any plantation at any given moment there were always several laid up for sickness, real and pretended, a tactic planters were ultimately helpless to counteract. If conditions persisted, or when personal relations between a slave and his owner or overseer became extremely strained—as when a slave felt himself unjustly punished—bondsmen often ran away.

Runaways

Slave runaways were a perennial problem for southern planters. Over the course of the slave-plantation system in the South the nature of runaways and their destinations changed, but in the antebellum period, after the spread of cotton and sugar cultivation, bondsmen ran away for three general reasons. Probably most common and of least worry to owners were those who in response to a real or felt injustice ran away for a short period simply to deprive the owner of a portion of the slave's labor. After all, here was a way for a slave to exert himself, to thwart his owner's intentions, to make a statement about his rights even if it came at some eventual cost to himself. Periodically when an owner or overseer forced slaves to work too hard or on the accepted weekend off (usually Saturday afternoon and Sunday), punished one unjustly, blamed one unfairly, or insulted a specially favored or skilled slave, the offended bondsman would disappear for several days or for three or four weeks.

Masters sometimes came to accept with a shrug this type of protest, knowing the absent slave would soon reappear, having in the meantime been living probably on the fringes of the plantation, maybe even slipping back to the quarters at night for food. Usually when the runaway did return he would receive a whipping or some other punishment, but occasionally owners disregarded the infraction of their rules and welcomed the runaway's return without disciplinary measures. This kind of commonplace running away was not a threat to the institution of slavery. The runaways themselves were protesting less the institution itself than invasions of their perceived rights as slaves. Owners seldom hunted for, probably never advertised for, such absent—not escaped—slaves. Because such limited running away was an accepted if unconscious method for aggrieved or angered slaves to work out their feelings in a bold but, from the owner's view, safe and harmless form, it no doubt relieved tensions, allowed resentments on both sides to cool, and incidentally reduced the possibility that hidden or suppressed rage might build to explosive levels.

While temporary running away was in effect a safety valve, a second common reason for running away represented a longer-term threat to slavery. The separation of slave families caused many bondsmen to leave their plantations in an effort to reunite with loved ones. Even if runaways of this kind eventually returned to their owners, the absence was often long enough to persuade the owner to place advertisements for their return in local newspapers. These advertisements, written as accurately as possible in hopes that the described slave would be located, frequently included hints that the runaway had joined his spouse or children at a certain location. Perhaps there is no stronger indication of the strength and resiliency of family ties among bondsmen than these efforts against all obstacles to see once again kin separated by distance. Even when runaways like these were recaptured and returned to their owners, the more realistic owners frequently would sell them to someone living in the vicinity of the loved one, knowing full well that the bonds of affection were stronger than discipline. Certainly many callous sellers and buyers of men disdained any human sympathies, but just as many—for reasons of practicality if not humanity—tried not to separate families unless in their view economic necessity required them to do so. Slavery's defenders as well as its critics recognized that the separation of families was a moral sore spot in the theoretical justification of bondage, and for that reason very seldom were small children parted from their mothers. Nevertheless, the trauma associated with sales of whatever nature forced many slaves to risk great danger and even greater hardships to see once more the faces of dear ones stolen away from them.

Despite the various factors that minimized slave rebellion and running away, there were nonetheless always situations, personality clashes, misunderstandings that drove slaves to cast aside their doubts and fears and escape to freedom. Often slaves who could not endure their bondage any longer but recognized the futility of individual violence or the inhospitableness of the countryside simply ran away to southern cities where they blended into the sizable free black population and disappeared. Skilled, articulate slaves, well-versed in the ways and expectations of their masters, were at the same time those most able to direct a potential slave insurrection and those most able, and likely, to succeed and even prosper as free blacks in Richmond, Charleston, or New Orleans. In yet another way southern cities, by offering a refuge to highly skilled slave runaways, helped defuse the potential for rebellion that might destroy the institution of bondage. Permanent slave escapees, then, whether they fled north or to southern cities to gain their freedom, had the ironic effect of making the existing system of slavery more stable by depriving the larger population of bondsmen of their most vocal, most able leaders.

Individual Acts of Rebellion

While slave owners often convinced themselves that the possibilities of large-scale slave insurrection were remote and failed to recognize the intent of resistance present in malingering and short-term running away, they realized that there were lethal individualistic ways of rebelling. Slaves were often suspected of arson and poisoning, in part because the causes of destructive fires and fatal diseases were so often mysterious. There are of course recorded instances of bondsmen using either of these to strike back at their owners, and surely both were successfully employed occasionally without raising undue suspicions. Contemporaries seem sometimes to have become almost hysterical over the imagined presence of vindictive slaves behind every unexplained fire or death. It would be a mistake, however, to follow the lead of overwrought, guilt-ridden slave owners. Sparks from fireplaces, poorly constructed chimneys, accidents associated with the smoking of meat or drying of tobacco, spontaneous combustion, and a lengthy list of barely understood and misdiagnosed diseases were probably more often at the bottom of sudden fires and unexplained illnesses.

Most Slaves Were Realistic About Their Situation

The absence of a tradition of armed slave uprisings in the Old South in no way supports the old myth of Sambo, the contented slave. Certainly there were passive, fawning, irresponsible, childlike Sambos, but they must have been but a fraction of the slave population. Far more common were the realistic slaves, men and women who knew they had to accept at least the physical constraints of bondage, who had a healthy sense of the possible and for whom family concerns were restraints against self-destructive rage. Whether it was understood or not, the vital Afro-American culture protected realistic slaves from being dehumanized; their culture provided them alternative ways of viewing life and did not allow the white man to control their inner world of values and dreams. By having something of their own to hold to, most bondsmen survived slavery, bending when survival dictated but not letting their spirit be broken.

They learned by necessity to cope with their existence, being by turns passive and assertive; knowing when to fawn and dissemble and when to protest; knowing how to get by guile what they had to have and how to avoid punishment. This indispensable know-how was transmitted from parents to children in a variety of ways. Whites, who seldom could see beyond their slaves' black faces, comprehended them all as Sambos, but again and again, when pushed too far, slaves resisted with a firmness and forthrightness that surprised their masters. To suppress their guilt over slave-holding, most southern whites tried desperately to convince themselves that blacks were a permanent child-race who needed and preferred slavery. When time after time slaves reacted with a maturity and boldness that should have called the racial stereotype into question, whites instead suspected outside forces—abolitionists, the example of free blacks, emancipationist literature—at work.

These realistic slaves represented the huge middle range of character types; at the opposite end of the spectrum from true Sambos were an equally small number of true rebels who with every fiber of their being rejected enslavement. Slave parents, knowing the consequence of attitudes of this kind, would try to dissuade their children from conspicuous rebellion. If the warnings were of no avail, sooner or later rebels were usually killed or suffered such brutality that their spirit was permanently broken, with suicide or self-mutilation sometimes the ultimate result. Too much attention has been focused on Sambos and rebels; most slaves were neither, though they could be a little of both as the occasion required.

With the invention of the cotton gin in 1793, the closing of the foreign slave trade in 1808, and the opening of the Old Southwest to the expansion of slavery after 1815, the political and economic foundations of the cotton kingdom were laid. The Revolutionary era imperceptibly merged into the Old South, with the institution of slavery like a giant black glacier inexorably spreading across the land, grinding down the rocks of resistance along the way and changing the entire social and cultural landscape in its wake. Nothing and no one remained untouched across the face of the South. Only a cataclysmic civil war could wrench blacks out of bondage and transform even incompletely a land so marked by natural beauty and human tragedy.

CHAPTER 3

Abolitionists and Their Opponents

# Chapter Preface

American abolitionists' long crusade to end slavery stands out as one of the nation's most inspiring social movements. However, the abolitionist movement never spoke with a single, unified voice. In fact, some of the movement's most significant impediments were its own internal divisions. In 1844 newspaper editor Jonathan B. Turner wrote in the *Illinois Statesman* that "there has already arisen so many various [abolitionist] sects . . . that the term 'abolition' like the term 'orthodox' really means nothing more than that a man may believe 'some things as well as others,' provided he sticks hard to the name." Abolitionists had many different ideas about how to achieve abolition and how the slaves, once they were freed, should be treated.

One of the main divisions was between those who favored gradual emancipation and those who favored the immediate abolition of slavery. Gradual emancipation had been the norm in the Northern states during the earliest phases of the abolitionist movement, during the eighteenth century when several Northern states instituted plans for freeing slaves over a period of several years, in some cases compensating slaveholders for their loss. However, the 1793 invention of the cotton gin made slaves more vital than ever to the Southern economy, deflating abolitionists' hopes that slavery might gradually fade away in the South. Opponents of slavery instead began calling for immediate abolition. They were inspired by Great Britain's abolition of slavery in 1833, which came in response to abolitionist pressure for immediate emancipation.

By the 1830s immediate abolition was the main goal of the most vocal abolitionists. However, not everyone who opposed slavery believed in racial equality. A significant faction of abolitionists believed that slavery should be abolished but that whites and free blacks would not be able to live together in peace. They promoted the return of free blacks to Africa. Even within this group there was a division between those who simply wanted to give free blacks the opportunity to migrate and those who wanted to expel free blacks from the United States. Members of each group, including statesmen such as James Monroe, Andrew Jackson, James Madison, Daniel Webster, and Henry Clay, came together in 1817 to found the American Colonization Society, which, over the next three decades, sent more than two thousand former slaves to Liberia in western Africa. However, colonization was always a controversial plan among abolitionists.

Perhaps the most significant division among abolitionists was a fundamental disagreement on how best to achieve emancipation. In one camp were those who favored political action—working "within the system." Political abolitionists included Frederick Douglass, a former slave turned writer and orator; and James Birney, a former slaveholder who, in 1840, ran as the presidential candidate for the antislavery Liberty Party. In a second camp were those who eschewed political action on the grounds that the U.S. government had become hopelessly corrupt in condoning slavery. They believed that abolitionists should instead focus on agitation—using oratory and writing to attack slavery and its defenders, arouse public interest in abolition, and persuade Americans that slavery was wrong.

The abolitionist tactic of agitation is primarily associated with William Lloyd Garrison, who began publishing his antislavery newspaper the *Liberator* in 1831. Religious revivalism was sweeping through the Northern states at the time, and Garrison embraced the view that slavery was a widespread national sin. As historian Larry Gara explains,

> Perhaps more than any other leader, Garrison shifted the crusade from gradualism to immediatism, and with others he led a devastating attack against colonization as a solution to the race problem which would become more acute with emancipation. Garrison's uncompromising language, his rejection of political action, . . . and his espousal of such causes as women's rights and nonresistance made him an unacceptable leader to many who were active in the cause, and led to many factional divisions. . . . Yet he remained a significant symbol of the antislavery crusade.

Garrison's and other agitators' inflammatory attacks on slavery exacerbated the growing hostility between North and South and alienated many moderate political abolitionists whose efforts often relied on compromise with proslavery groups. Many historians have questioned whether Garrison and his followers' extremism helped or hindered the abolitionist movement. As one abolitionist lamented in 1849, "The abolitionists are split to pieces . . . each piece imagining itself holier than the others."

The factional disputes within the abolitionist movement were abandoned at the end of the Civil War when emancipation was finally realized. Throughout the North many people who had avoided the label *abolitionist* embraced it. The leaders of the movement were hailed as heroes, and charges that some of them had been fanatics were quickly forgotten. As Gara writes, "The descendants of abolitionists glowed with pride over the courageous deeds of their forbears. Such second generation admirers seldom made distinctions between varieties of abolitionist thought."

Later generations *have* examined the different varieties of abolitionist thought and have gained insight from the many different arguments used both to defend and attack the abolitionist cause. These arguments are explored in the following chapter.

Viewpoint 1

"Human prudence forbids that we should precipitately engage in a work of such hazard as a general and simultaneous emancipation."

Emancipation Should Be Gradual

St. George Tucker

St. George Tucker was a judge in the Virginia Supreme Court of Appeals and a professor of law at the College of William and Mary in Williamsburg, Virginia. In 1796 he published a long pamphlet called *A Dissertation on Slavery* in which he proposed a plan for the gradual abolition of slavery in Virginia. Ultimately, Tucker's pamphlet had little impact, and his proposals were never enacted in Virginia, but his arguments provide insight into why some Southerners opposed slavery.

In arguing for gradual emancipation, Tucker was motivated primarily by the fear of slave insurrection and violence. Like many Southerners, he had been greatly influenced by slave insurrections in the French colony of St. Dominique (now Haiti), which began in 1791 and ultimately led to the independence of Haiti and the abolition of slavery there. One feature of Tucker's plan was the denial of all political rights to freed slaves.

Tucker did not believe that free blacks and whites could coexist peacefully, and he opposed immediate emancipation on the grounds that freed blacks might attack their former masters. He

St. George Tucker, *A Dissertation on Slavery: With a Proposal for the Gradual Abolition of It, in the State of Virginia.* Philadelphia: M. Carey, 1796.

131

believed that forcing freed slaves to migrate to Africa or to live on a separate colony within the United States was both unjust and impractical, but nevertheless hoped that denying political rights to blacks would encourage them to settle outside Virginia.

In the preceding enquiry into the absolute rights of the citizens of united America, we must not be understood as if those rights were equally and universally the privilege of all the inhabitants of the United States, or even of all those, who may challenge this land of freedom as their native country. Among the blessings which the Almighty hath showered down on these states, there is a large portion of the bitterest draught that ever flowed from the cup of affliction. Whilst America hath been the land of promise to Europeans, and their descendants, it hath been the vale of death to millions of the wretched sons of Africa. The genial light of liberty, which hath here shone with unrivalled lustre on the former, hath yielded no comfort to the latter, but to them hath proved a pillar of darkness, whilst it hath conducted the former to the most enviable state of human existence. Whilst we were offering up vows at the shrine of Liberty, and sacrificing hecatombs upon her altars; whilst we swore irreconcilable hostility to her enemies, and hurled defiance in their faces; whilst we adjured the God of Hosts to witness our resolution to live free, or die, and imprecated curses on their heads who refused to unite with us in establishing the empire of freedom; we were imposing upon our fellow men, who differ in complexion from us, a slavery, ten thousand times more cruel than the utmost extremity of those grievances and oppressions, of which we complained.

An Arduous Task

The extirpation [destruction] of slavery from the United States, is a task equally arduous and momentous. To restore the blessings of liberty to near a million of oppressed individuals, who have groaned under the yoke of bondage, and to their descendants, is an object, which those who trust in Providence, will be convinced would not be unaided by the divine Author of our being, should

we invoke his blessings upon our endeavours. Yet human prudence forbids that we should precipitately engage in a work of
such hazard as a general and simultaneous emancipation. The
mind of man must in some measure be formed for his future condition. The early impressions of obedience and submission, which
slaves have received amongst us, and the no less habitual arro-
gance and assumption of superiority, among the whites, con-
tribute, equally, to unfit the former for *freedom*, and the latter for
equality. To expel them all at once, from the United States, would
in fact be to devote them only to a lingering death by famine, by
disease, and other accumulated miseries. . . . To retain them
among us, would be nothing more than to throw so many of the
human race upon the earth without the means of subsistence: they
would soon become idle, profligate, and miserable. Unfit for their
new condition, and unwilling to return to their former laborious
course, they would become the caterpillars of the earth, and the
tigers of the human race. The recent history of the French West
Indies exhibits a melancholy picture of the probable consequences
of a general, and momentary emancipation in any of the states,
where slavery has made considerable progress. In Massachusetts
the abolition of it was effected by a single stroke; a clause in their
constitution: but the whites at that time, were as sixty-five to one,
in proportion to the blacks. The whole number of free persons in
the United States, south of Delaware state, are 1,233,829, and there
are 648,439 slaves; the proportion being less than two to one. Of
the cultivators of the earth in the same district, it is probable that
there are four slaves for one free white man.—To discharge the
former from their present condition, would be attended with an
immediate general famine, in those parts of the United States,
from which not all the productions of the other states, could deliver them; similar evils might reasonably be apprehended from
the adoption of the measure by any one of the southern states; for
in all of them the proportion of slaves is too great, not to be attended with calamitous effects, if they were immediately set free.
These are serious, I had almost said unsurmountable obstacles, to
a general, simultaneous emancipation.

There are other considerations not to be disregarded. A great
part of the *property* of individuals consists in *slaves*. The laws have

sanctioned this species of property. Can the laws take away the property of an individual without his own consent, or without a *just compensation*? Will those who do not hold slaves agree to be taxed to make this compensation? Creditors also, who have trusted their debtors upon the faith of this visible property will be defrauded. If justice demands the emancipation of the slave, she, also, *under these circumstances*, seems to plead for the owner, and for his creditor. The claims of nature, it will be said are stronger than those which arise from social institutions, only. I admit it, but nature also dictates to us to provide for our *own* safety, and authorizes all *necessary* measures for that purpose. And we have shewn that our own security, nay, our very existence, might be endangered by the hasty adoption of any measure for the *immediate* relief of the *whole* of this unhappy race. Must we then quit the subject, in despair of the success of any project for the amendment of their, as well as our own, condition! I think not.—Strenuously as I feel my mind opposed to a simultaneous emancipation, for the reasons already mentioned, the abolition of slavery in the United States, and especially in that state, to which I am attached by every tie that nature and society form, is *now* my *first*, and will probably be my last, expiring wish. But here let me avoid the imputation of inconsistency, by observing, that the abolition of slavery may be effected without the *emancipation* of a single slave; without depriving any man of the *property* which he *possesses*, and without defrauding a creditor who has trusted him on the faith of that property. The experiment in that mode has already been begun in some of our sister states. Pennsylvania, under the auspices of the immortal Franklin, begun the work of gradual abolition of slavery in the year 1780, by enlisting nature herself, on the side of humanity. Connecticut followed the example four years after. New-York very lately made an essay which miscarried, by a very inconsiderable majority. Mr. Jefferson informs us, that the committee of revisors, of which he was a member, had prepared a bill for the emancipation of all slaves born after passing that act. This is conformable to the Pennsylvania and Connecticut laws.—Why the measure was not brought forward in the general assembly I have never heard. Possibly because objections were foreseen to that part of the bill which relates to the disposal of the blacks, af-

Emancipation Must Accommodate Slave Owners

Frances Wright was a feminist and reformer. In A Plan for the Gradual Abolition of Slavery in the United States Without Danger of Loss to the Citizens of the South, *published in 1825, she urged Congress to set aside tracts of land on which freed slaves could settle. In December 1825 she founded an experimental community in Tennessee called Nashoba, where she allowed slaves she owned to work off the cost of their purchase in order to gain their freedom. She wanted to demonstrate that slaves working for their freedom would work harder than other slaves. Wright hoped that the enterprise would be profitable and, if adopted elsewhere, would hasten the demise of slavery. Due to several factors, including poor management by Wright and a scandal over charges of free love among the Nashoba residents, the experiment was abandoned after five years.*

It appears superfluous, in proposing a plan for the general abolition of slavery from the United States, to observe upon the immensity of the evil, and the gloomy prospect of dangers it presents to the American people—disunion, bloodshed, servile wars of extermination, horrible in their nature and consequences, and disgraceful in the eyes of the civilized world.

It is conceived that any plan of emancipation, to be effectual, must consult at once the pecuniary [financial] interests and prevailing opinions of the southern planters, and bend itself to the existing laws of the southern states. In consequence, it appears indispensable, that emancipation be connected with colonization, and that it demand no pecuniary sacrifice from existing slaveholders, and entail no loss of property on their children.

Frances Wright, *A Plan for the Gradual Abolition of Slavery in the United States Without Danger of Loss to the Citizens of the South*, 1825.

ter they had attained a certain age. It certainly seems liable to many, both as to the policy and the practicability of it.

A Separate Colony for Freed Slaves?

To establish such a colony in the territory of the United States, would probably lay the foundation of intestine wars, which would terminate only in their extirpation, or final expulsion. To attempt it in any other quarter of the globe would be attended with the utmost cruelty to the colonists, themselves, and the destruction of their whole race. If the plan were at this moment in operation, it would require the annual exportation of 12,000 persons. This requisite number must, for a series of years be considerably increased, in order to keep pace with the increasing population of those people. In twenty years it would amount to upwards of twenty thousand persons; which is half the number which are now supposed to be annually exported from Africa.—Where would a fund to support this expence be found? Five times the present revenue of the state would barely defray the charge of their passage. Where provisions for their support after their arrival? Where those necessaries which must preserve them from perishing?—Where a territory sufficient to support them?—Or where could they be received as friends, and not as invaders? To colonize them in the United States might seem less difficult. If the territory to be assigned them were beyond the settlements of the whites, would they not be put upon a forlorn hope against the Indians? Would not the expence of transporting them thither, and supporting them, at least for the first and second year, be also far beyond the revenues and abilities of the state? The expence attending a small army in that country hath been found enormous. To transport as many colonists, annually, as we have shewn were necessary to eradicate the evil, would probably require five times as much money as the support of such an army. But the expence would not stop there: they must be assisted and supported at least for another year after their arrival in their new settlements. Suppose them arrived. Illiterate and ignorant as they are, is it probable that they would be capable of instituting such a government, in their new colony, as would be necessary for their own internal happiness, or to secure them from destruction from without? European emigrants, from whatever country they arrive, have been accustomed to the restraint of laws, and the respect for government. These people, accustomed to be ruled with a rod of iron, will not easily submit to milder restraints. They would become hordes of vagabonds, robbers and murderers. Without the aids of an enlightened policy, morality, or religion, what else could be expected from their still savage state, and debased condition?

"But why not retain and *incorporate the blacks into the state*?" This question has been well answered by Mr. Jefferson, and who is there so free from prejudices among us, as candidly to declare that he has none against such a measure? The recent scenes transacted in the French colonies in the West Indies are enough to make one shudder with the apprehension of realizing similar calamities in this country. Such probably would be the event of an attempt to smother those prejudices which have been cherished for a period of almost two centuries. Those who secretly favour, whilst they affect to regret, domestic slavery, contend that in abolishing it, we must also abolish that scion from it which I have denominated *civil* slavery. That there must be no distinction of rights; that the descendants of Africans, as men, have an equal claim to all civil rights, as the descendants of Europeans; and upon being delivered from the yoke of bondage have a right to be admitted to all the privileges of a citizen.—But have not men when they enter into a state of society, a right to admit, or exclude any description of persons, as they think proper? If it be true, as Mr. Jefferson seems to suppose, that the Africans are really an inferior race of mankind, will not sound policy advise their exclusion from a society in which they have not yet been admitted to participate in civil rights; and even to guard against such admission, at any future period, since it may eventually depreciate the whole national character? And if prejudices have taken such deep root in our minds, as to render it impossible to eradicate this opinion, ought not so general an error, if it be one, to be respected? Shall we not relieve the necessities of the naked diseased beggar, unless we will invite him to a seat at our table; nor afford him shelter from the inclemencies of the night air, unless we admit him also to share our bed? To deny that we ought to abolish slavery, without incorporating the Negroes into the state, and admitting them to a full participation of all our civil and social rights, appears to me to rest upon a similar foundation. The experiment so far as it has been already made amongst us, proves that the emancipated blacks are not ambitious of civil rights. To prevent the generation of such an ambition, appears to comport with sound policy; for if it should ever rear its head, its partizans, as well as its opponents, will be enlisted by nature herself, and always ranged in formidable array against each other. We must therefore endeavour to find some middle course, between the tyrannical and iniquitous [unjust] policy which holds so many human creatures in a state of grievous bondage; and that which would turn loose a numerous, starving, and enraged banditti, upon the innocent descendants of their former oppressors. *Nature, time*, and *sound policy* must co-operate with each other to produce such a change: if either be neglected, the work will be incomplete, dangerous, and not improbably destructive.

A Plan of Gradual Abolition

The plan therefore which I would presume to propose for the consideration of my countrymen is such, as the number of slaves, the difference of their nature, and habits, and the state of agriculture, among us, might render it *expedient*, rather than *desirable* to adopt: and it would partake partly of that proposed by Mr. Jefferson, and adopted in other states; and partly of such cautionary restrictions, as a due regard to situation and circumstances, and even to *general* prejudices, might recommend to those, who engage in so arduous, and perhaps unprecedented an undertaking.

1. Let every female born after the adoption of the plan be free, and transmit freedom to all her descendants, both male and female.

2. As a compensation to those persons, in who families such females, or their descendants may be born, for the expence and trouble of their maintenance during infancy, let them serve such persons until the age of twenty-eight years: let them then receive twenty dollars in money, two suits of clothes, suited to the season, a hat, a pair of shoes, and two blankets. If these things be not voluntarily done, let the county courts enforce the performance, upon complaint.

3. Let all Negroe children be registered with the clerk of the county or corporation court, where born, within one month af-

ter their birth: let the person in whose family they are born take a copy of the register, and deliver it to the mother, or if she die to the child, before it is of the age of twenty-one years. Let any Negroe claiming to be free, and above the age of puberty, be considered as of the age of twenty-eight years, if he or she be not registered, as required.

4. Let all such Negroe servants be put on the same footing as white servants and apprentices now are, in respect to food, raiment, correction, and the assignment of their service from one to another.

5. Let the children of Negroes and mulattoes, born in the families of their parents, be bound to service by the overseers of the poor, until they shall attain the age of twenty-one years. Let all above that age, who are not housekeepers, nor have voluntarily bound themselves to service for a year before the first day of February annually, be then bound for the remainder of the year by the overseers of the poor. Let the overseers of the poor receive fifteen per cent. of their wages, from the person hiring them, as a compensation for their trouble, and ten per cent. per annum out of the wages of such as they may bind apprentices.

6. If at the age of twenty-seven years, the master of a Negroe or mulattoe servant be unwilling to pay his freedom dues, above mentioned, at the expiration of the succeeding year, let him bring him into the county court, clad and furnished with necessaries as before directed, and pay into court five dollars, for the use of the servant, and thereupon let the court direct him to be hired by the overseers of the poor for the succeeding year, in the manner before directed.

7. Let no Negroe or mulattoe be capable of taking, holding, or exercising, any public office, freehold, franchise or privilege, or any estate in lands or tenements, other than a lease not exceeding twenty-one years.—Nor of keeping, or bearing arms, unless authorized so to do by some act of the general assembly, whose duration shall be limited to three years. Nor of contracting matrimony with any other than a Negroe or mulattoe; nor be an attorney; nor be a juror; nor a witness in any court of judicature, except against, or between Negroes and mulattoes. Nor be an executor or administrator; nor capable of making any will or testament; nor maintain any real action; nor be a trustee of lands or tenements himself, nor

any other person to be a trustee to him or to his use.

8. Let all persons born after the passing of the act, be considered as entitled to the same mode of trial in criminal cases, as free Negroes and mulattoes are now entitled to.

Encouraging Freed Slaves to Deport

The restrictions in this place may appear to favour strongly of prejudice: whoever proposes any plan for the abolition of slavery, will find that he must either encounter, or accommodate himself to prejudice.—I have preferred the latter; not that I pretend to be wholly exempt from it, but that I might avoid as many obstacles as possible to the completion of so desirable a work, as the abolition of slavery. Though I am opposed to the banishment of the Negroes, I wish not to encourage their future residence among us. By denying them the most valuable privileges which civil government affords, I wished to render it their inclination and their interest to seek those privileges in some other climate. There is an immense unsettled territory on this continent [the Louisiana Purchase] more congenial to their natural constitutions than ours, where they may perhaps be received upon more favourable terms than we can permit them to remain with us. Emigrating in small numbers, they will be able to effect settlements more easily than in large numbers; and without the expence or danger of numerous colonies. By releasing them from the yoke of bondage, and enabling them to seek happiness wherever they can hope to find it, we surely confer a benefit, which no one can sufficiently appreciate, who has not tasted of the bitter curse of compulsory servitude. By excluding them from offices, the seeds of ambition would be buried too deep, ever to germinate: by disarming them, we may calm our apprehensions of their resentments arising from past sufferings; by incapacitating them from holding lands, we should add one inducement more to emigration, and effectually remove the foundation of ambition, and party-struggles. Their personal rights, and their property, though limited, would whilst they remain among us be under the protection of the laws; and their condition not at all inferior to that of the *labouring* poor in most other countries. Under such an arrangement we might reasonably hope, that time would either remove from us a race of men, whom we wish not to incorporate with us, or obliterate those prejudices, which now form an obstacle to such incorporation.

But it is not from the want of liberality to the emancipated race of blacks that I apprehend the most serious objections to the plan I have ventured to suggest. Those slave holders (whose numbers I trust are few) who have been in the habit of considering their fellow creatures as no more than cattle, and the rest of the brute creation, will exclaim that they are to be deprived of their *property*, without compensation. Men who will shut their ears against this moral truth, that all men are by nature *free*, and *equal*, will not even be convinced that they do not possess a *property* in an *unborn* child: they will not distinguish between allowing to *unborn* generations the absolute and unalienable rights of human nature, and taking away that which they *now possess*; they will shut their ears against truth, should you tell them, the loss of the mother's labour for nine months, and the maintenance of a child for a dozen or fourteen years, is amply compensated by the services of that child for as many years more, as he has been an expence to them. But if the voice of reason, justice and humanity be not stifled by sordid avarice, or unfeeling tyranny, it would be easy to convince even those who have entertained such erroneous notions, that the right of one man over another is neither founded in nature, nor in sound policy. That it cannot extend to those *not in being;* that no man can in reality be *deprived* of what he doth not possess: that fourteen years labour by a young person in the prime of life, is an ample compensation for a few months of labour lost by the mother, and for the maintenance of a child, in that coarse homely manner that Negroes are brought up: And lastly, that a state of slavery is not only perfectly incompatible with the principles of government, but with the safety and security of their masters. History evinces [demonstrates] this.

Viewpoint 2

"I utterly reject, as delusive and dangerous in the extreme, every plea which justifies a procrastinated and an indefinite emancipation."

Emancipation Should Be Immediate

William Lloyd Garrison

William Lloyd Garrison was one of the most prominent leaders of the abolitionist movement. From 1831 to 1865 he edited and published the *Liberator*, a newspaper noted for its uncompromising abolitionist stance. In 1833 he helped found the American Anti-Slavery Society and was its president from 1843 to 1865.

Garrison's most notable contribution to the abolitionist movement was his complete rejection of gradual abolition. Whereas more moderate abolitionists had hoped that slavery might slowly fade away in the South, Garrison argued that slavery was clearly evil and that plans for gradual abolition were thus morally wrong. Garrison also fiercely attacked the colonization movement, which held that freed blacks should be encouraged or forced to migrate to Africa. In the following excerpt from his 1832 book *Thoughts on African Colonization*, Garrison outlines his view that plans for gradual emancipation are fundamentally unjust.

William Lloyd Garrison, *Thoughts on African Colonization, or An Impartial Exhibition of the Doctrines, Principles, and Purposes of the American Colonization Society, Together with Resolutions, Addresses, and Remonstrances of the Free People of Color.* Boston: Garrison and Knapp, 1832.

Since the deception practised upon our first parents by the old serpent, there has not been a more fatal delusion in the minds of men than that of the gradual abolition of slavery. *Gradual* abolition! do its supporters really know what they talk about? Gradually abstaining from what? From sins the most flagrant, from conduct the most cruel, from acts the most oppressive! Do colonizationists mean, that slave-dealers shall purchase or sell a few victims less this year than they did the last? that slave-owners shall liberate one, two or three out of every hundred slaves during the same period? that slave-drivers shall apply the lash to the scarred and bleeding backs of their victims somewhat less frequently? Surely not—I respect their intelligence too much to believe that they mean any such thing. But if any of the slaves should be exempted from sale or purchase, why not all? if justice require the liberation of the few, why not of the many? if it be right for a driver to inflict a number of lashes, how many shall be given? Do colonizationists mean that the practice of separating the husband from the wife, the wife from the husband, or children from their parents, shall come to an end by an almost imperceptible process? or that the slaves shall be defrauded of their just remuneration, less and less every month or every year? or that they shall be under the absolute, irresponsible control of their masters? Oh no! I place a higher value upon their good sense, humanity and morality than this! Well, then, they would immediately break up the slave traffic—they would put aside the whip—they would have the marriage relations preserved inviolate—they would not separate families—they would not steal the wages of the slaves, nor deprive them of personal liberty! This is abolition—*immediate abolition.* It is simply declaring that slave owners are bound to fulfill—now, without any reluctance or delay—the golden rule, namely, to do as they would be done by; and that, as the right to be free is inherent and inalienable in the slaves, there ought now to be a disposition on the part of the people to break their fetters. All the horrid spectres which are conjured up, on this subject, arise from a confusion of the brain, as much as from a corruption of the heart.

I utterly reject, as delusive and dangerous in the extreme, every plea which justifies a procrastinated and an indefinite emancipation, or which concedes to a slave owner the right to hold his slaves as *property* for any limited period, or which contends for the gradual preparation of the slaves for freedom; believing all such pretexts to be a fatal departure from the high road of justice into the bogs of expediency, a surrender of the great principles of equity, an indefensible prolongation of the curse of slavery, a concession which places the guilt upon any but those who incur it, and directly calculated to perpetuate the thraldom [enslavement] of our species.

Immediate abolition does not mean that the slaves shall immediately exercise the right of suffrage, or be eligible to any office, or be emancipated from law, or be free from the benevolent restraints of guardianship. We contend for the immediate personal freedom of the slaves, for their exemption from punishment except where law has been violated, for their employment and reward as free laborers, for their exclusive right to their own bodies and those of their own children, for their instruction and subsequent admission to all the trusts, offices, honors and emoluments of intelligent freemen. Emancipation will increase and not destroy the value of their labor; it will also increase the demand for it. Holding out the stimulus of good treatment and an adequate reward, it will induce the slaves to toil with a hundred fold more assiduity and faithfulness. Who is so blind as not to perceive the peaceful and beneficial results of such a change? The slaves, if freed, will come under the watchful cognizance of law; they will not be idle, but *avariciously* industrious; they will not rush through the country, firing dwellings and murdering the inhabitants; for freedom is all they ask—all they desire—the obtainment of which will transform them from enemies into friends, from nuisances into blessings, from a corrupt, suffering and degraded, into a comparatively virtuous, happy and elevated population.

Nor does immediate abolition mean that any compulsory power, other than moral, should be used in breaking the fetters of slavery. It calls for no bloodshed, or physical interference; it jealously regards the welfare of the planters; it simply demands an entire revolution in public sentiment, which will lead to better conduct, to contrition for past crimes, to a love instead of a fear of justice, to a reparation of wrongs, to a healing of breaches, to a suppression of revengeful feelings, to a quiet, improving, prosperous state of society! . . .

[Friends of the Colonization Society say] 'To say that immediate emancipation will only increase the wretchedness of the slaves, and that we must pursue a system of *gradual* abolition, is to present to us the double paradox, that we must continue to do evil, in order to cure the evil which we are doing; and that we must continue to be unjust, and to do evil, that good may come.' The fatal error of *gradualists* lies here: They talk as if the friends of abolition contended only for the emancipation of the slaves, without specifying or caring what should be done with or for them! as if the planters were invoked to cease from one kind of villany, only to practise another! as if the manumitted [freed] slaves must necessarily be driven out from society into the wilderness, like wild beasts! This is talking nonsense: it is a gross perversion of reason and common sense. Abolitionists have never said, that mere manumission would be doing justice to the slaves: they insist upon a remuneration for years of unrequited toil, upon their employment as free laborers, upon their immediate and coefficient instruction, and upon the exercise of a benevolent supervision over them on the part of their employers. They declare, in the first place, that to break the fetters of the slaves, and turn them loose upon the country, without the preservative restraints of law, and destitute of occupation, would leave the work of justice only half done; and, secondly, that it is absurd to suppose that the planters would be wholly independent of the labor of the blacks—for they could no more dispense with it next week, were emancipation to take place, than they can to-day. The very ground which they assume for their opposition to slavery,—that it necessarily prevents the improvement of its victims,—shows that they contemplate the establishment of schools for the education of the slaves, and the furnishing of productive employment, immediately upon their liberation. If this were done, none of the horrors which are now so feelingly depicted, as the attendants of a sudden abolition, would ensue.

Emancipation and Education

But we are gravely told that education must *precede* emancipation. The logic of this plea is, that intellectual superiority justly gives one man an oppressive control over another! Where would such a detestable principle lead but to practices the most atrocious, and results the most disastrous, if carried out among ourselves? Tell us, ye hair-splitting sophists, the exact quantum of knowledge which is necessary to constitute a freeman. If every dunce should be a slave, your servitude is inevitable; and richly do you deserve the lash for your obtuseness. Our white population, too, would furnish blockheads enough to satisfy all the classical kidnappers in the land.

The reason why the slaves are so ignorant, is because they are held in bondage; and the reason why they are held in bondage, is because they are so ignorant! They ought not to be freed until they are educated; and they ought not be educated, because on the acquisition of knowledge they would burst their fetters! Fine logic, indeed! How men, who make any pretensions to honesty or common sense, can advance a paradox like this, is truly inexplicable. . . .

It is said, by way of extenuation, that the present owners of slaves are not responsible for the origin of this system. I do not arraign them for the crimes *of their ancestors*, but for the constant perpetration and extension of similar crimes. The plea that the evil of slavery was entailed upon them, shall avail them nothing: in its length and breadth it means that the robberies of one generation justify the robberies of another! that the inheritance of stolen property converts it into an honest acquisition! that the atrocious conduct of their fathers exonerates them from all accountability, thus presenting the strange anomaly of a race of men incapable of incurring guilt, though daily practising the vilest deeds! Scarcely any one denies that blame attaches somewhere: the present generation throws it upon the past—the past, upon its predecessor—and thus it is cast, like a ball, from one to another, down to the first importers of the Africans! 'Can that be *innocence* in the temperate zone, which is the *acme of all guilt* near the equator? Can that be *honesty* in one meridian of longitude, which, at one hundred degrees east, is the *climax of injustice?*' Sixty thousand infants, the offspring of slave-parents, are annually born in this country, and doomed to remediless bondage. Is it not as atrocious a crime to kidnap these, as to kidnap a similar number on the coast of Africa?

Faulty Emancipation Plans

It is said, moreover, that we ought to legislate prospectively, on this subject; that the fetters of the present generation of slaves cannot be broken; and that our single aim should be, to obtain the freedom of their offspring, by fixing a definite period after which none shall be born slaves. But this is inconsistent, inhuman and unjust. The following extracts from the speech of the Rev. Dr. Thomson are conclusive on this point:

> 'It amounts to an indirect sanction of the continued slavery of all who are now alive, and of all who may be born before the period fixed upon. This is a renunciation of the great moral principles upon which the demand for abolition proceeds. It consigns more than 800,000 human beings to bondage and oppression, while their title to freedom is both indisputable and acknowledged. . . .

> 'Supposing all children born after January 1, 1831, were declared free, how are they to be educated? That they may be prepared for the enjoyment of that liberty with which you have invested them, they must undergo a particular and appropriate training. So say the *gradualists.* Very well; under whom are they to get this training? Are they to be separated from their parents? Is that dearest of natural ties to be broken asunder? Is this necessary for your plan? And are not you thus endeavoring to cure one species of wickedness by the instrumentality of another? But if they are to be left with their parents and brought up under their care, then either they will be imbued with the faults and degeneracies that are characteristic of slavery, and consequently be as unfit for freedom as those who have not been disenthralled: or they will be well nurtured and well instructed by their parents, and this implies a confession that their parents themselves are sufficiently prepared for liberty, and that there is no good reason for withholding from them, the boon that is bestowed upon their children.

> 'Whatever view, in short, we take of the question, the prospective plan is full of difficulty or contradictions, and we are made more sensible than ever that there is nothing left for us,

but to take the consistent, honest, uncompromising course of demanding the abolition of slavery with respect to the present, as well as to every future generation of the negroes in our colonies.'

We are told that 'it is not right that men should be free, when their freedom will prove injurious to themselves and others.' This has been the plea of tyrants in all ages. If the immediate emancipation of the slaves would prove a curse, it follows that slavery is a blessing; and that it cannot be unjust, but benevolent, to defraud the laborer of his hire, to rank him as a beast, and to deprive him of his liberty. But this, every one must see, is at war with common sense, and avowedly doing evil that good may come. This plea must mean, either that a state of slavery is more favorable to the growth of virtue and the dispensation of knowledge than a state of freedom—(a glaring absurdity)—or that an immediate compliance with the demands of justice would be most unjust—(a gross contradiction.)

It is boldly asserted by some colonizationists, that '*the negroes are happier when kept in bondage,*' and that 'the condition of the great mass of emancipated Africans is one in comparison with which the condition of the slaves is *enviable.*' What is the inference? Why, either that slavery is not oppression—(another paradox)—or that real benevolence demands the return of the free people of color to their former state of servitude. Every kidnapper, therefore, is a true philanthropist! Our legislature should immediately offer a bounty for the body of every free colored person! The colored population of Massachusetts, at $200 per each man, woman and child, would bring at least *one million three hundred thousand dollars.* This sum would seasonably replenish our exhausted treasury. The whole free colored population of the United States, at the same price, (which is a low estimate,) would be worth *sixty-five millions of dollars!!* Think how many churches this would build, schools and colleges establish, beneficiaries educate, missionaries support, bibles and tracts circulate, railroads and canals complete, &c. &c. &c. !!! . . .

Those who prophesy evil, and only evil, concerning immediate abolition, absolutely disregard the nature and constitution of man, as also his inalienable rights, and annihilate or reverse the causes and effects of human action. They are continually fearful lest the slaves, in consequence of their grievous wrongs and intolerable sufferings, should attempt to gain their freedom by revolution; and yet they affect to be equally fearful lest a general emancipation should produce the same disastrous consequences. How absurd! They *know* that oppression must cause rebellion; and yet they pretend that a removal of the cause will produce a bloody effect! This is to suppose an effect without a cause, and, of course, is a contradiction in terms. Bestow upon the slaves personal freedom, and all motives for insurrection are destroyed. Treat them like rational beings, and you may surely expect rational treatment in return: treat them like beasts, and they will behave in a beastly manner.

Besides, precedent and experience make the ground of abolitionists invulnerable. In no single instance where their principles have been adopted, has the result been disastrous or violent, but beneficial and peaceful even beyond their most sanguine expectations. The immediate abolition of slavery in Mexico, in Colombia, and in St. Domingo, was eminently preservative and useful in its effects. . . . According to the Anti-Slavery Reporter for January, 1832, three thousand prize negroes at the Cape of Good Hope had received their freedom—four hundred in one day; 'but not the least difficulty or disorder occurred: servants found masters, masters hired servants—all gained homes, and at night scarcely an idler was to be seen.'

These and many other similar facts show conclusively the safety of immediate abolition. Gradualists can present, in abatement of them, nothing but groundless apprehensions and criminal distrust. The argument is irresistible.

Viewpoint 3

"We consider [emancipation] . . . so fraught with danger and mischief both to the whites and blacks . . . that we cannot . . . give it our sanction."

Emancipation Is Impractical

Thomas R. Dew

The following viewpoint is excerpted from Thomas R. Dew's book *Review of the Debate in the Virginia Legislature of 1831 and 1832*. Dew was a professor of political economy and law at the College of William and Mary in Williamsburg, Virginia, and his book was a response to the Virginia legislature's recent debate over whether to abolish slavery. The debate—the last time in the South the idea of abolishing slavery was seriously considered—came in response to the slave rebellion led by lay preacher Nat Turner in October 1831, in which approximately sixty whites were killed.

In his book, Dew praised the Virginia legislature's decision to not abolish slavery and staunchly defended slavery as a positive good. In the excerpts presented here, Dew argues that emancipation would harm Virginia's economy, since slavery was a profitable institution. He also argues that slaves, if freed, would be prone to idleness and perhaps even violence against whites. He concludes that the social and economic disruptions of emancipation greatly outweigh whatever benefits it might confer.

Thomas R. Dew, *Review of the Debate in the Virginia Legislature of 1831 and 1832*. Richmond, VA: T.W. White, 1832.

We shall now . . . inquire seriously and fairly, whether there be any means by which we may get rid of slavery. . . .

We will examine first, those schemes which propose abolition and deportation; and secondly, those which contemplate emancipation without deportation.

1st. *Emancipation and Deportation.*—In the late Virginia Legislature, where the subject of slavery underwent the most thorough discussion, all seemed to be perfectly agreed in the necessity of removal in case of emancipation. Several members from the lower counties, which are deeply interested in this question, seemed to be sanguine [positive] in their anticipations of the final success of some project of emancipation and deportation to Africa, the original home of the negro. "Let us translate them," said one of the most respected and able members of the Legislature, (Gen. Broadnax,) "to those realms from which, in evil times, under inauspicious influences, their fathers were unfortunately abducted. . . ."

Deportation Is Impractical

Fortunately for reason and common sense, all these projects of deportation may be subjected to the most rigid and accurate calculations, which are amply sufficient to dispel all doubt, even in the minds of the most sanguine, as to their practicability.

We take it for granted, that the right of the owner to his slave is to be respected, and, consequently, that he is not required to emancipate him, unless his full value is paid by the State. Let us, then, keeping this in view, proceed to the very simple calculation of the expense of emancipation and deportation in Virginia. The slaves, by the last census (1830,) amounted within a small fraction to 470,000; the average value of each one of these is, $200; consequently, the whole aggregate value of the slave population of Virginia, in 1830, was $94,000,000; and allowing for the increase since, we cannot err far in putting the present value at $100,000,000. The assessed value of all the houses and lands in the State, amounts to $206,000,000, and these constitute the material items in the wealth of the State, the whole personal property besides bearing but a very small proportion to the value of slaves, lands, and houses. Now, do not these very simple statistics speak volumes upon this subject? It is gravely recommended to the State of Virginia to give up a species of property which constitutes nearly one-third of the wealth of the whole state, and almost one-half of that of Lower Virginia, and with the remaining two-thirds to encounter the additional enormous expense of transportation and colonization on the coast of Africa. But the loss of $100,000,000 of property is scarcely the half of what Virginia would lose, if the immutable laws of nature could suffer (as fortunately they cannot) this tremendous scheme of colonization to be carried into full effect. . . .

Slaves Give Virginia Value

It is, in truth, the slave labor in Virginia which gives value to her soil and her habitations; take away this, and you pull down the Atlas that upholds the whole system; eject from the State the whole slave population, and we risk nothing in the prediction, that on the day in which it shall be accomplished, the worn soils of Virginia would not bear the paltry price of the government lands in the West, and the Old Dominion will be a "waste howling wilderness";—"the grass shall be seen growing in the streets, and the foxes peeping from their holes."

But the favorers of this scheme say they do not contend for the sudden emancipation and deportation of the whole black population; they would send off only the increase, and thereby keep down the population to its present amount, while the whites, increasing at their usual rate, would finally become relatively so numerous as to render the presence of the blacks among us for ever afterwards entirely harmless. This scheme, which at first, to the unreflecting, seems plausible, and much less wild than the project of sending off the whole, is nevertheless impracticable and visionary, as we think a few remarks will prove. It is computed that the annual increase of the slaves and free colored population of Virginia is about six thousand. Let us first, then, make a calculation of the expense of purchase and transportation. At $200 each, the six thousand will amount in value to $1,200,000. At $30 each, for transportation, which we shall soon see is too little, we have the whole expense of purchase and transportation $1,380,000, an expense to be annually incurred by Virginia to keep down her black population to its present amount. And let us ask, is there anyone who can seriously argue that Virginia can incur such an annual expense as this for the next twenty-five or fifty years, until the whites have multiplied so greatly upon the blacks, as, in the *opinion* of the *alarmists*, for ever to quiet the fears of the community? Vain and delusive hope, if any were ever wild enough to entertain it! Poor old Virginia! . . .

It is almost useless to inquire whether this deportation of slaves to Africa would, as some seem most strangely to anticipate, invite the whites of other States into the Commonwealth. Who would be disposed to enter a State with worn out soil, and a black population mortgaged to the payment of millions *per annum*, for the purpose of emancipation and deportation, when in the West the most luxuriant soils, unincumbered with heavy exactions, could be purchased for the paltry sum of $1.25 per acre?

Where, then, is that multitude of whites to come from, which the glowing fancy of orators has sketched out as flowing into and filling up the *vacuum* created by the removal of slaves? . . .

Seeing, then, that the effort to send away the increase, on even the present increase of our slaves, must be vain and fruitless, how stupendously absurd must be the project, proposing to send off the whole increase, so as to keep down the negro population at its present amount! There are some things which man, arrayed in all his "brief authority," cannot accomplish, and this is one of them. . . .

Emancipation without Deportation.—We candidly confess, that we look upon this last mentioned scheme as much more practicable, and likely to be forced upon us, than the former. We consider it, at the same time, so fraught with danger and mischief both to the whites and blacks—so utterly subversive of the welfare of the slaveholding country, in both an economical and moral point of view, that we cannot, upon any principle of right or expediency, give it our sanction. . . .

Much was said in the Legislature of Virginia about superiority of free labor over slave, and perhaps, under certain circumstances, this might be true; but, in the present instance, the question is between *the relative amounts of labor which may be obtained from slaves before and after their emancipation.* Let us, then, first commence with our country, where, it is well known to everybody, that slave labor is vastly more efficient and productive than the labor of free blacks.

A Worthless Class

Taken as a whole class, the latter [free blacks] must be considered the most worthless and indolent of the citizens of the United States. It is well known that throughout the whole extent of our Union, they are looked upon as the very *drones* and *pests* of society. Nor does this character arise from the disabilities and disfranchisement by which the law attempts to guard against them. In the non-slaveholding States, where they have been more elevated by law, this kind of population is in a worse condition, and much more troublesome to society, than in the slaveholding, and especially in the planting States. Ohio, some years ago, formed a sort of land of promise for this deluded class, to which many have repaired from the slaveholding States,—and what has been the consequence? They have been most harshly expelled from that State, and forced to take refuge in a foreign land. Look through the Northern States, and mark the class upon whom the eye of the police is most steadily and constantly kept—see with what vigilance and care they are hunted down from place to place—and you cannot fail to see that idleness and improvidence are at the root of all their misfortunes. Not only does the experience of our own country illustrate this great fact, but others furnish abundant testimony. . . .

In the free black, the principle of idleness and dissipation triumphs over that of accumulation and the desire to better our condition; the animal part of the man gains the victory over the moral, and he, consequently, prefers sinking down into the listless, inglorious repose of the brute creation, to rising to that energetic activity which can only be generated amid the multiplied, refined, and artificial wants of civilized society. The very conception which nine slaves in ten have of liberty, is that of idleness and sloth with the enjoyment of plenty; and we are not to wonder that they should hasten to practice upon their theory so soon as liberated. But the experiment has been sufficiently tried to prove most conclusively that the free black will work nowhere except by compulsion. . . .

The great evil, however, of these schemes of emancipation, remains yet to be told. They are admirably calculated to excite plots, murders and insurrections; whether gradual or rapid in their operation, this is the inevitable tendency. In the former case, you disturb the quiet and contentment of the slave who is left unemancipated; and he becomes the midnight murderer to gain that fatal freedom whose blessings he does not comprehend. In the latter case, want and invidious distinction will prompt to revenge. Two totally different races, as we have before seen, cannot easily harmonize together, and although we have no idea that any organized plan of insurrection or rebellion can ever secure for the black the superiority, even when free, yet his idleness will produce want and worthlessness, and his very worthlessness and degradation will stimulate him to deeds of rapine and vengeance; he will oftener engage in plots and massacres, and thereby draw down on his devoted head, the vengeance of the provoked whites. But one limited massacre is recorded in Virginia history; let her liberate her slaves, and every year you would hear of insurrections and plots, and every day would perhaps record a murder; the melancholy tale of Southampton would not alone blacken the page of our history, and make the tender mother shed the tear of horror over her babe as she clasped it to her bosom; others of a deeper dye would thicken upon us; those regions where the brightness of polished life has dawned and brightened into full day, would relapse into darkness, thick and full of horrors. . . .

The Evils of Slavery

Injustice and Evils of Slavery.—1st. It is said slavery is wrong, in the *abstract* at least, and contrary to the spirit of Christianity. To this we answer as before, that any question must be determined by its circumstances, and if, as really is the case, we cannot get rid of slavery without producing a greater injury to both the masters and slaves, there is no rule of conscience or revealed law of God which *can* condemn us. The physician will not order the spreading cancer to be extirpated, although it will eventually cause the death of his patient, because he would thereby hasten the fatal issue. So, if slavery had commenced even contrary to the laws of God and man, and the sin of its introduction rested upon our heads, and it was even carrying forward the nation by slow degrees to final ruin— yet, if it were *certain* that an attempt to remove it would only hasten and heighten the final catastrophe—that it was, in fact, a "vulnus immedicabile" on the body politic which no legislation could safely remove, then we would not only not be found to attempt the extirpation, but we would stand guilty of a high offence in the sight of both God and man, if we should rashly make the effort. But the original sin of introduction rests not on our heads, and we shall soon see that all those dreadful calamities which the false prophets of our day are pointing to, will never, in all probability, occur.

But it is time to bring this long article to a close; it is upon a subject which we have most reluctantly discussed; but, as we have already said, the example was set from a higher quarter; the seal has been broken, and we therefore determined to enter fully into the discussion. If our positions be true, and it does seem to us they may be sustained by reasoning almost as conclusive as the demonstrations of the mathematician, it follows, that the time for emancipation has not yet arrived, and perhaps it never will. We hope, sincerely, that the intelligent sons of Virginia will ponder before they move—before they enter into a scheme which will destroy more than half Virginia's wealth, and drag her down from her proud and elevated station among the mean things of the earth,— and when, Samson-like, she shall, by this ruinous scheme, be shorn of all her power and all her glory, the passing stranger may at some future day exclaim,

The Niobe of nations—there she stands, "Friendless and helpless in her voiceless woe."

Once more, then, do we call upon our statesmen to pause, ere they engage in this ruinous scheme. The power of man has limits, and he should never attempt impossibilities. We do believe it is beyond the power of man to separate the elements of our population, even if it were desirable. The deep and solid foundations of society cannot be broken up by the vain *fiat* of the legislator. ... We must recollect, in fine, that our own country has waded through two dangerous wars—that the thrilling eloquence of the Demosthenes of our land has been heard with rapture, exhorting to death, rather than slavery,—that the most liberal principles have ever been promulgated and sustained, in our deliberate bodies, and before our judicial tribunals—and the whole has passed by without breaking or tearing asunder the elements of our social fabric. Let us reflect on these things, and learn wisdom from experience; and know that the relations of society, generated by the *lapse of ages*, cannot be altered in a *day*.

Viewpoint 4

"Not one case of insurrection or of bloodshed has ever been heard of, as the result of emancipation."

Emancipation Is Practical

Lydia Maria Child

Lydia Maria Child was a writer and abolitionist who first gained popularity in the 1820s through her children's fiction (she is remembered today for the Thanksgiving poem "Over the River and Through the Wood") and her series of domestic advice books, which included *The American Frugal Housewife*. In 1833 she published a popular but controversial antislavery tract titled "An Appeal in Favor of That Class of Americans Called African," which depressed the sales of her other books. She continued to write abolitionist editorials in newspapers, and later embraced a variety of causes including women's rights and Indian welfare.

The following viewpoint is excerpted from Child's 1839 book *Anti-Slavery Catechism*, in which she attempts to put a moderate face on abolitionism. She emphasizes the practical benefits of emancipation and uses a question-and-answer format to deal with criticisms of abolitionism. Child rejects claims that emancipation will lead to violence and that free blacks cannot take care of themselves.

Lydia Maria Child, *Anti-Slavery Catechism*. Newburyport, MA: Charles Whipple, 1839.

Q. But don't you think it would be dangerous to turn the slaves at once loose upon the community?

A. The abolitionists never desired to have them turned loose. They wish to have them governed by salutary laws, so regulated as effectually to protect both master and slave. They merely wish to have the power of punishment transferred from individuals to magistrates; to have the sale of human beings cease; and to have the stimulus of *wages* applied, instead of the stimulus of the *whip*. The relation of master and laborer might still continue; but under circumstances less irksome and degrading to both parties. Even that much abused animal the jackass can be made to travel more expeditiously by suspending a bunch of turnips on a pole and keeping them before his nose, than he can by the continual application of the whip; and even when human beings are brutalized to the last degree, by the soul-destroying system of slavery, they have still sense enough left to be more willing to work two hours for twelve cents than to work one hour for nothing.

Q. I should think this system, in the long run, must be an unprofitable one.

A. It is admitted to be so. Southerners often declare that it takes six slaves to do what is easily performed by half the number of free laborers. . . .

Q. But the masters say the negroes would cut their throats, if they were emancipated.

A. It is safer to judge by uniform experience than by the assertions of the masters, who, even if they have no intention to deceive, are very liable to be blinded by having been educated in the midst of a bad system. Listen to facts on this subject. On the 10th of October, 1811, the Congress of Chili decreed that every child born after that day should be free. In April, 1812, the government of Buenos Ayres ordered that every child born after the 1st of January, 1813, should be free. In 1821, the Congress of Colombia emancipated all slaves who had borne arms in favor of the Republic, and provided for the emancipation, in eighteen years, of the whole slave population of 900,000. In September, 1829, the government of Mexico granted immediate and entire emancipation to every slave. In all these instances, *not one case of insurrection or of bloodshed has ever been heard of, as the result of emancipation.*

In St. Domingo no measures were taken gradually to fit the slaves for freedom. They were suddenly emancipated during a civil war, and armed against British invaders. They at once ceased to be property, and were recognized as human beings. Col. Malefant, who resided on the island, informs us, in his Historical and Political History of the Colonies, that, "after this public act of emancipation, the negroes remained quiet both in the south and west, and they continued to work upon all the plantations. The colony was flourishing. The whites lived happily and in peace upon their estates, and the negroes continued to work for them." General Lacroix, in his Memoirs of St. Domingo, speaking of the same period says: "The colony marched as by enchantment towards its ancient splendor; cultivation prospered; every day produced perceptible proofs of its progress." This prosperous state of things lasted about eight years, and would perhaps have continued to the present day, had not Bonaparte, at the instigation of the old French planters, sent an army to deprive the blacks of the freedom they had used so well. The enemies of abolition are always talking of the horrors of St. Domingo, as an argument to prove that emancipation is dangerous; but historical facts prove that the effort to *restore slavery* occasioned all the bloodshed in that island; while *emancipation produced only the most peaceful and prosperous results.* . . .

Q. But they say the British have had difficulties in their West Indies.

A. The enemies of the cause have tried very hard to get up a "raw-head and bloody-bones" story; but even if you take their own accounts, you will find that they have not been able to adduce any instances of violence in support of their assertions. . . .

Q. Yet people are always saying that free negroes cannot take care of themselves.

A. It is because people are either very much prejudiced or very ignorant on the subject. In the United States, colored persons have scarcely any chance to rise. They are despised, and abused, and discouraged, at every turn. In the slave States they are subject to laws nearly as oppressive as those of the slave. They are whipped or imprisoned, if they try to learn to read or write; they are not allowed to testify in court; and there is a general disposition not to encourage them by giving them employment. In addition to this, the planters are very desirous to expel them from the State, partly because they are jealous of their influence upon the slaves, and partly because those who have slaves to let out, naturally dislike the competition of the free negroes. But if colored people are well treated, and have the same inducements to industry as other people, they work as well and behave as well. A few years ago the Pennsylvanians were very much alarmed at the representations that were made of the increase of pauperism from the ingress of free negroes. A committee was appointed to examine into the subject, and it was ascertained that the colored people not only supported their own poor, but paid a considerable additional sum towards the support of white paupers.

Q. I have heard people say that the slaves would not take their freedom, if it were offered to them.

A. I sincerely wish they would offer it. I should like to see the experiment tried. If the slaves are so well satisfied with their condition, why do they make such severe laws against running away? Why are the patroles [*sic*] on duty all the time to shoot every negro who does not give an account of himself as soon as they call to him? Why, notwithstanding all these pains and penalties, are their newspapers full of advertisements for runaway slaves? If the free negroes are so much worse off than those in bondage, why is it that their laws bestow freedom on any slave, "who saves his master or mistress's life, or performs any meritorious service to the State?" That must be a very bad country where the law stipulates that *meritorious* actions shall be rewarded by making a man more unhappy than he was before! . . .

Q. Some say that these people are naturally inferior to us; and that the shape of their skulls proves it.

A. If I believed that the colored people were naturally inferior to the whites, I should say that was an additional reason why we ought to protect, instruct, and encourage them. No consistent republican will say that a strong-minded man has a right to oppress those less gifted than himself. Slave-holders do not seem to think the negroes are so stupid as not to acquire knowledge, and make use of it, if they could get a chance. If they do think so, why do their laws impose such heavy penalties on all who attempt to give them any education? Nobody thinks it necessary to forbid the promulgation of knowledge among monkeys. If you believe the colored race are naturally inferior, I wish you would read the history of Toussaint L'Ouverture, the Washington of St. Domingo. Though perfectly black, he was unquestionably one of the greatest and best men of his age. I wish you would hear Mr. Williams of New York, and Mr. Douglass of Philadelphia preach a few times, before you hastily decide concerning the capacity of the colored race for intellectual improvement. As for the shape of their skulls, I shall be well satisfied if our Southern brethren will emancipate all the slaves who have *not* what is called the "African conformation.". . . .

Q. But would you at once give so many ignorant creatures political power, by making them voters?

A. That would be for the wisdom of legislators to decide; and they would probably decide that it would not be judicious to invest emancipated slaves with the elective franchise; for though it is not their fault that they have been kept brutally ignorant, it unfits them for voters. . . .

Q. You know that abolitionists are universally accused of wishing to promote the amalgamation of colored and white people.

A. This is a false charge, got up by the enemies of the cause, and used as a bugbear to increase the prejudices of the community. By the hue and cry that is raised on the subject, one would really suppose that in this free country a certain set of men had power to compel their neighbors to marry contrary to their own inclination. The abolitionists have never, by example, writing, or conversation, endeavored to connect amalgamation with the subject of abolition. When their enemies insist upon urging this silly and unfounded objection, they content themselves with replying, "If there be a natural antipathy between the races, the antipathy will protect itself. If such marriages are contrary to the order of Providence, we certainly may trust Providence to take care of the matter. It is a poor compliment to the white young men to be so afraid that the moment we allow the colored ones to be educated, the girls will all be running after them.". . . .

Q. Is there any truth in the charge that you wish to break down all distinctions of society; and introduce the negroes into our parlors?

A. There is not the slightest truth in this charge. People have pointed to an ignorant shoe-black, and asked me whether I would invite him to visit my house. I answered, "No; I would not do so if he were a white man; and I should not be likely to do it, merely because he was black." An educated person will not naturally like to associate with one who is grossly ignorant. It may be no merit in one that he is well-informed, and no fault of the other that he is ignorant; for these things may be the result of circumstances, over which the individual had no control; but such people will not choose each other's society merely from want of sympathy. For these reasons, I would not select an ignorant man, of any complexion, for my companion; but when you ask me whether that man's children shall have as fair a chance as my own, to obtain an education, and rise in the world, I should be ashamed of myself, both as a Christian and a republican, if I did not say, yes, with all my heart.

Overcoming Prejudice

Q. But do you believe that prejudice against color ever can be overcome?

A. Yes, I do; because I have faith that all things will pass away, which are not founded in reason and justice. In France and England, this prejudice scarcely exists at all. Their noblemen would never dream of taking offence because a colored gentleman sat beside them in a stage-coach, or at the table of an hotel. Be assured, however, that the abolitionists have not the slightest wish to force you to give up this prejudice. If, after conscientious examination, you believe it to be right, cherish it; but do not adhere to it merely because your neighbors do. Look it in the face—apply the golden rule—and judge for yourself. The Mahometans really think they could not eat at the same table with a Christian, without pollution; but I have no doubt the time will come when this prejudice will be removed. The old feudal nobles of England would not have thought it possible that their descendants could live in a community, where they and their vassals were on a perfect civil equality; yet the apparent impossibility has come to pass, with advantage to many, and injury to none. When we endeavor to conform to the spirit of the gospel, there is never any danger that it will not lead us into paths of peace. . . .

Q. But if the system works so badly in every respect, why are people so unwilling to give it up?

A. Human nature is willing to endure much, rather than relinquish unbridled licentiousness and despotic control. The emperor of Russia, and the pachas [sic] of Egypt would be reluctant to abridge their own power, for the sake of introducing a system of things more conducive to the freedom, virtue and happiness of their subjects. They had rather live in constant fear of the poisoned bowl and the midnight dagger, than to give up the pleasant exercise of tyranny, to which they have so long been accustomed. In addition to this feeling, so common to our nature, there are many conscientious people, who are terrified at the idea of emancipation. It has always been presented to them in the most frightful colors; and bad men are determined, if possible, to prevent the abolitionists from proving to such minds that *the dangers of insurrection all belong to slavery, and would cease when slavery was abolished.*

At the North, the apologists of slavery are numerous and virulent, because their *interests* are closely intertwined with the pernicious system. Inquire into the private history of many of the men, who have called meetings against the abolitionists—you will find that some manufacture negro cloths for the South—some have sons who sell these cloths—some have daughters married to slaveholders—some have plantations and slaves mortgaged to them—some have ships employed in Southern commerce—and some candidates for political offices would bow until their backbones were broken, to obtain or preserve Southern influence. The Southerners understand all this perfectly well, and despise our servility, even while they condescend to make use of it.

One great reason why the people of this country have not thought and felt right on this subject, is that all our books, newspapers, almanacs and periodicals, have combined to represent the colored race as an inferior and degraded class, who never could be made good and useful citizens. Ridicule and reproach have been abundantly heaped upon them; but their virtues and their sufferings have found few historians. The South has been well satisfied with such a public sentiment. It sends back no echo to disturb their consciences, and it effectually rivets the chain on the necks of their vassals. In this department of service, the Colonization Society has been a most active and zealous agent.

Abolitionists and Violence

Q. But some people say that all the mobs, and other violent proceedings, are to be attributed to the abolitionists.

A. They might as well charge the same upon St. Paul, when his fearless preaching of the gospel brought him into such imminent peril, that his friends were obliged to "let him down over the wall in a basket," to save his life. As well might St. Stephen have been blamed for the mob that stoned him to death. With the same justice might William Penn have been called the cause of all the violent persecutions against the Quakers. When principles of truth are sent out in the midst of a perverse generation, they *always* come "not to bring peace, but a sword." The abolitionists have offered violence to no man—they have never attempted to stop the discussions of their opponents; but have, on the contrary, exerted themselves to obtain a candid examination of the subject on all sides. They merely claim the privilege of delivering peaceful addresses at orderly meetings, and of publishing what they believe to be facts, with an honest desire to have them tested by the strictest ordeal of truth.

Viewpoint 5

"[William Lloyd Garrison] was a man of distinctly narrow limitations among the giants of the antislavery movement."

William Lloyd Garrison Made a Minor Contribution to the Abolitionist Movement

Dwight Lowell Dumond

William Lloyd Garrison was one of the most prominent leaders of the abolitionist movement. He founded the abolitionist newspaper the *Liberator* in 1831 and helped found the American Anti-Slavery Society in 1833. However, many historians have depicted Garrison in a negative light, maintaining that his extreme views on the sinfulness of slavery alienated Northerners and Southerners alike and thus hindered the abolitionist movement. Historian Dwight Lowell Dumond, for example, in the following excerpt from his 1961 book *Antislavery: Crusade for Freedom in America*, describes Garrison as a zealot whose contributions to

Dwight Lowell Dumond, *Antislavery: The Crusade for Freedom in America.* Ann Arbor: University of Michigan Press, 1961.

the abolitionist movement were far less constructive than those of more conservative and less visible opponents of slavery.

Garrison was twenty-two years of age [in 1827]. He had learned the printer's trade on the Newburyport *Herald*, then had edited and published the *Free Press*. He published here the first writings of young John Greenleaf Whittier. In January 1828 he became editor of the *Boston National Philanthropist*, a temperance paper. Three months later he listened to [abolitionist Benjamin] Lundy's discussion of slavery. Lundy was back in Boston again in August 1828, and Garrison heard him speak again, this time at the Federal Street Baptist Church. Shortly afterward, Garrison assumed the editorship of the Bennington (Vt.) *Journal of the Times* on condition he might discuss antislavery, temperance, peace, and moral reform as well as politics. This was the beginning of his career as a reformer and Christian anarchist. He was at this point, with reference to slavery, a Lundy colonizationist, urging the formation of antislavery societies, the petitioning of Congress for abolition of slavery in the District of Columbia, and transportation elsewhere of liberated slaves and free Negroes willing to go. He circulated and sent to Congress a petition for abolition in the District signed by 2,352 citizens of Vermont. This petition, written by himself, reveals one of his great weaknesses, about which we shall say much later: ignorance of American history, constitutional law, and previous antislavery tradition and literature. Speaking of slavery in the District of Columbia, he said: "The proposed abolition will interfere with no State rights. Beyond this District, Congress has no power to legislate—so far, at least, as slavery is concerned; but it can, by one act, efface this foul stain from our national reputation." Quite obviously he was not familiar with the long history of the territorial question.

Garrison then gave a fourth of July address in Boston in 1829 which showed him to be at the age of twenty-four strongly opposed to slavery, but still a colonizationist and in favor of gradual emancipation by action of the slave states. He argued that the free states were "constitutionally involved in the guilt of slavery, by adhering to a national compact that sanctions it"; that Negroes could be elevated to intelligent citizenship by freedom and education; that the churches were neglecting their responsibility to the slaves; that the vast majority of the Negroes, slave and free, were born in the United States and were entitled to all the privileges of citizenship; that the variance between our professed devotion to liberty and equality and our oppression of the Negroes was shameful; that the free states might rightfully demand gradual emancipation; and that all citizens should assist in systematically promoting colonization through societies, private contributions, and congressional action. . . .

Garrison Repudiates Colonization

In June 1830, he spoke in Philadelphia and New York to the members and friends of the societies for the abolition of slavery and improvement of free colored people, and in New Haven to the Negro parishioners of Simeon S. Jocelyn, a white home missionary. He then spoke in his home town of Newburyport in September 1830 and in Boston. Even those who recognized his talents and complete devotion to the cause were disturbed by his strong language, and particularly by his denunciation of the churches. On the other hand, some men who did not fully agree with him, but recognized his ability, gave him support, among them [abolitionist] Samuel J. May.

The first issue of the *Liberator* contained the words, many times repeated, "I will be as harsh as truth, and as uncompromising as justice. On this subject, I do not wish to think, or speak, or write, with moderation." Far more important, however, was the following repudiation of gradual emancipation: "In Park Street Church, on the Fourth of July, 1829, in an address on slavery, I unreflectingly assented to the popular but pernicious [dangerous] doctrine of *gradual* abolition. I seize this opportunity to make a full and unequivocal recantation, and thus publicly [*sic*] to ask pardon of my God, of my country, and of my brethren the poor slaves, for having uttered a sentiment so full of timidity, injustice, and absurdity."

Garrison's complete repudiation of colonization came more slowly, but with equal finality. Speaking before the Negroes of New York and Philadelphia in June 1831, he quite frankly condemned colonizationists for their harsh treatment of Negroes, particularly their refusal to provide employment and education in order to drive them out of the country, for intensifying prejudice by repeatedly asserting that Negroes were incapable of elevation to equality with the whites, and for their apologies for slavery. Two years before he had urged Negroes to go to Liberia; now he said: "Every intelligent man of color, whom the Colonization Society induces to go to Liberia, ought to be considered as a traitor to your cause." This was the sort of free and easy imperiousness which caused men to hate him. On the other hand, there was a large element of truth in his sweeping indictment that followed: "Now," said he, "what a spectacle is presented to the world! . . . The story is proclaimed in our pulpits, in our state and national assemblies, in courts of law, in religious and secular periodicals,— among all parties, and in all quarters of the country,—that there is a *moral incapacity* in the people to do justly, to love mercy, and to walk uprightly—that they must always be the enemies and oppressors of the colored people—that no love of liberty, no dictate of duty, no precept of republicanism, no dread of retribution, no claim of right, no injunction of gospel, can possibly persuade them to do unto their colored countrymen, as they would that they should do unto them in a reversal of circumstances.". . .

The *Liberator* and the American Anti-Slavery Society

William Lloyd Garrison emerged as one of the most controversial figures of the antislavery movement. Opposition to publication of the *Liberator* was not slow to develop during the summer of 1831. It was neither more nor less than that which [abolitionists James G.] Birney and [Elijah] Lovejoy were to experience in Ohio and Illinois. Considering the rather more incisive language of Garrison, the publication of [David] Walker's *Appeal* in Boston, and the Nat Turner insurrection, both at about the same time that the *Liberator* was founded, it was less than might have been expected; and it unquestionably was softened by Garrison's strong emphasis upon temperance, peace, and women's rights. So far as slavery was concerned he favored immediate emancipation and opposed colonization. He favored emancipation in the District of Columbia and abolition of the three-fifths rule in apportionment.

He vigorously denied that there could be such a thing as property rights in man or that men could be denied natural rights because of race or color. He was opposed to violence and insurrection.

There was nothing new in any of the above. Garrison was sustained in his tenacious adherence to the principles by [abolitionist John] Rankin's *Letters* which he republished in the *Liberator* and by George Bourne's *The Book and Slavery Irreconcilable.* Fifteen persons assembled in Boston on November 13, 1831, about a year after the *Liberator* was launched, for the purpose of organizing an antislavery society. The basis of discussion was Elizabeth Heyrich's principle of immediate emancipation. Six persons refused to endorse it. Another meeting of ten persons assembled on December 16, and out of this meeting developed the New England Anti-Slavery Society. It was a fancy name for a feeble organization, because the Constitution, published in the *Liberator*, February 18, 1832, was signed by only a dozen men. Membership increased very slowly, and after three years the name was changed to the Massachusetts Anti-Slavery Society. . . .

Garrison's Positive and Negative Contributions

Long and careful study of [Garrison's] writings, speeches, and relationships in comparison with other men in the movement leads one to certain inescapable conclusions.

He had an ability to write. In fact, at times he wrote brilliantly. There was a certain positiveness, even a doctrinaire quality about his ideas, and a harshness, sometimes a fury, in his language. Slaveholders hated him because of it, but that was of little consequence. They hated anyone who spoke against slavery. What was its effect upon the progress of emancipation? The answer must be paradoxical. Nothing short of intense, uncompromising, even violent denunciation of slavery and of slaveholders would have aroused the country, but it alienated the support of some moderate men. It did not retard emancipation because there was nothing to retard. It did not evoke a violent defense of slavery because slaveholders had always been vehement in its defense. However, Garrison gloried in opposition, magnified it beyond reality, thought of himself as a potential martyr, and became insufferably arrogant at times in his treatment of other men, to the detriment of the cause.

He did not aid slaves to escape in the manner of Levi Coffin or a hundred other men. He did not establish schools and teach Negroes in the tradition of [Anthony] Benezet, as did Marius Robinson, Hiram Wilson, and others. He did not aid them in mastery of mechanical arts and agriculture as did Augustus Wattles. He did not brave the fury of countless mobs as did Theodore Weld, Henry B. Stanton, and Elijah Lovejoy. He did not write the solid treatises of antislavery literature. He did not aid the Negroes financially, rather he relied heavily upon *them* for support of his paper and purchase of his books. He did not provide legal assistance in cases of Negroes who were kidnapped or white men who were prosecuted for assisting fugitives. He did not engage in the furious contests in political campaigns and legislative halls as did Thomas Morris, James G. Birney, and Joshua Giddings. In fact, *he was a man of distinctly narrow limitations among the giants of the antislavery movement.* But he provided, in the *Liberator*, an opportunity for the Negro leaders to express their views and encourage their people. His strong, relentless championship of human rights; his refusal to recognize distinctions of color or race with respect to ability, achievement, and rights; his condemnation of every sort of injustice were an encouragement and a blessing to an oppressed people which can not be measured but was very great.

Finally, Garrison denounced the Constitution as a proslavery document. It was not—and was not intended to be—a proslavery document. In fact it provided ample scope for antislavery legislation by Congress. Garrison's intemperate language regarding the Constitution and government of the United States, and his ultimate refusal to vote because government rested upon force hurt the cause of emancipation. It was ill-considered and without justification. It played into the hands of the proslavery men. It was an obstacle to political action against slavery. It split the American Anti-Slavery Society, and ultimately the church associations of New England. It need not have done so had the colossal conceit of the man not led him to claim credit for almost everything that was done in the movement before 1840. He made a contribution. It was neither a large nor an overpowering one, and sometimes it was a negative one.

Viewpoint 6

"Garrison was a person of real historical importance, for he was a symbol to his generation of the moral and ideological conflict that took its final shape in the Civil War."

William Lloyd Garrison Made an Important Contribution to the Abolitionist Movement

Russel B. Nye

William Lloyd Garrison was one of the most controversial abolitionists of his day, and his legacy has become a topic of debate among modern historians. While many historians regard Garrison as an outspoken fanatic who overshadowed and alienated more moderate opponents of slavery, some historians have sought to rescue Garrison's place in history. In his book *William Lloyd Garrison and the Humanitarian Reformers*, Michigan State

Russel B. Nye, *William Lloyd Garrison and the Humanitarian Reformers.* Boston: Little, Brown and Company, 1955. Copyright © 1955 by Russel B. Nye. Reproduced by permission.

University professor Russel B. Nye offered a more sympathetic description of Garrison. In the excerpt reprinted here, Nye acknowledges that Garrison's uncompromising self-righteousness put him outside the mainstream abolitionist movement. However, Nye maintains that Garrison's outspokenness did much to make slavery a topic of intense national debate.

[W]illiam Lloyd] Garrison's mind worked on two levels, the moral and the practical. On the one, his approach to issues was determined by principle; on the other, by tactics and strategy. The level of his argument fluctuated, as it did during the Civil War when he scourged Lincoln on principles, yet pleaded the value of expediency. Fundamentally, his approach to things was simple and consistent. He judged everything by two standards of moral right—natural law as expressed in the Declaration of Independence, and Christian ethic as expressed in the Bible. To him these were essentially one, emanating from the same divine source. Any idea or institution which violated either, in part or whole, therefore was wrong. The final judgment rested with individual conscience, the roots of which lay in God. A world of conscience so rooted was Garrison's "kingdom to be established on earth," in which the individual's own soul became the arbiter of action and the judge of institutions—a kingdom in which men voluntarily ceased to sin, established justice, and worshiped God in a "magistracy of holiness and love."

Garrison's Religious Zeal

The central fact of Garrison's life was his religious faith. The Bible was the only book he ever really read, and his abolitionism itself sprang directly from his belief that slavery violated God's law. "It was not on account of your complexion or race, as a people, that I espoused your cause," he told a Negro meeting in Charleston in 1865, "but because you were the children of a common Father, created in the same divine image, having the same inalienable rights. . . ." Despite the charge of "infidelity" that followed him wherever he went, he was a rigidly religious man. The bland neutrality of nineteenth-century Unitarianism was not for him. The finespun speculations of New England transcendentalism lay beyond his capacity; even Lyman Beecher's brand of modified Calvinism was too soft. Instead he returned to an earlier, rigorous faith, straight from his Bible. In 1842, stung to exasperation by accusations of "infidelity," he published his creed in the *Liberator*:

> I believe that, in Jesus Christ, the believer is dead unto sin, and alive with God—that whosoever is born of God overcometh the world—that Christ is the end of the law for righteousness, to everyone who believeth. . . . I believe that priestcraft, and sectarianism, and slavery, and war, and everything that defileth or maketh a lie, are of the devil, and destined to an eternal overthrow.

The language was the language of the Old Testament, the spirit that of third-century Christianity. He had the zeal and fanaticism of a Biblical prophet, combined with apostolic dedication. His religion, he said, was "that of the Jewish religionists of eighteen centuries ago," and his God a Hebraic God who spoke directly to his conscience. Him and only Him would Garrison obey and call Master.

From this Godbased individualism flowed Garrison's revolt against manmade authority—abolition, disunion, pacifism, perfectionism, women's rights, and "infidelity." "Individual, personal effort"—he wrote—

> is the true foundation of all real prosperity in the social state, and all excellence of character. No form of Society can be devised which will release the individual from personal responsibility. . . . It would be the greatest curse that could be inflicted upon him.

An Uncompromising Idealist

Garrison thus did not belong in an age of conciliation and compromise, nor was he fitted for what his era called "the principle of association." He liked, he said, "causes which, being righteous, are unpopular, and struggling, in God's name, against wind and tide." With God and conscience on his side, turmoil was his natural element. "Hisses," he once said, "are music to my ears." Organizations strait-jacketed him; he accepted them only as utensils for his own use. Temperamentally he was a no-government man and his aversion to cooperation was as ingrained as Thoreau's.

Garrison was a true revolutionary individualist who accepted nothing beyond himself, no tradition or institution whose existence violated his own inner, higher law. There was something of the eighteenth-century rebel in him, and more of the seventeenth-century Puritan's self-righteous independence. Emerson, too, preached the sufficiency of self and the integrity of self-reliance as God-reliance, but Garrison's deity was no transcendental Oversoul. His was a stern, inflexible God of wrath and justice, his individualism a flinty, arrogant self-faith. Emerson's individualism was ascetic and intellectual; Garrison's was visceral, emotional. He could never have taken to the woods as Thoreau did. He was a social being, tied to humanity and incapable of acting without it. As Emerson shrewdly remarked, Garrison "would find nothing to do in a lonely world, or a world with half-a-dozen inhabitants."

Acting from his own driving religious faith and within the terms of his society, Garrison had every reason to be what he was—the Reformer Incarnate. He conceived himself to be the tool of God, his followers "soldiers of God" with "loins girt about with truth" and "feet shod with the preparation of the Gospel of peace." His aim was nothing less than "the emancipation of our whole race from the dominion of man, from the thraldom of self, from the government of brute force, from the bondage of sin." This was the New Jerusalem, the kingdom of God awaited by the Hebrew prophets. The complete freedom of man was to him the whole purpose of life, and he lived with singleminded devotion to it.

Those who accused Garrison of deserting the main battle of abolition for minor skirmishes failed to recognize that to Garrison no reform, however close to the lunatic fringe, was unrelated to the larger purpose. He was always, as he said late in life, interested in nothing less than "the redemption of the human race." If the human race needed redemption from slavery on the one hand and cigar-smoking on the other, there was no reason to neglect one crusade for another if both could proceed at once. Bronson Alcott, of all Garrison's contemporaries, understood the grand sweep of his design and saw what the others missed. He was, Alcott wrote in his journal, wholly "intent on the melioration of human woes and the eradication of human evils." Nothing else could satisfy him. Garrison was no intellectual, but a man of action. He never liked to speculate, and he had no reverence for reflection. Emerson once said that Garrison "neighed like a horse" when they discussed ideas. Unlike Emerson, Garrison never tried to search hard for truth, because he had it.

The moral self-righteousness that lay beneath Garrison's crusade for the kingdom of God on earth was difficult to accept. There was no vacillation in him, no gray in his thinking, only right and wrong, deep black and pure white. There could be no compromise with sin and only Garrison could define sin. To disagree with him was to disagree with Right personified. In the last analysis his final court of appeal was conscience, not mind. Moral judgment was his first and last line of defense, and for this reason it was almost impossible to persuade him he was wrong. Founded on God and conscience, his stand was impregnable.

Garrison's Self-Righteousness

This absolute self-confidence was one reason his band followed him with worship this side of idolatry. Garrison had no hesitations, no questionings, no doubts, and inspired the same self-assurance in others. His sincerity and courage attracted men so widely different as the gentle [Samuel J.] May, the urbane [Wendell] Phillips, the wildly unstable [Abigail Kelley] Foster, and the unpredictable [Elizur] Wright. Some of his twists and turns made his most ardent supporters swallow hard, but Garrison to the end of his life believed himself perfectly consistent and unassailably right. His enemies always respected his obstinate sincerity. They sometimes thought he was wrong, or arrogant, or unreasonable— but never insincere. He was capable of absolute identification with a principle. If he believed in an idea he would die for it, though it be ill-advised, wrong, or downright foolish. This monolithic self-confidence drew men to him.

Garrison's faith in himself made him unconsciously dictatorial. He genuinely considered himself a modest man, refusing personal praise and credit. Yet he constantly sought it with a real inward hunger. His personality felt a deep need for recognition. He never aspired to political office, though certainly after 1861 he could have had it. He paid little attention to money, security, or possessions. He simply neglected to write his memoirs when he could have made thousands, and the financial status of the *Liberator* was always more important to him than his own. But he was sure from the first that he was a man for the ages, and he felt compelled to keep reminding himself and others of the fact. His remarks in the *Liberator*, less than a year after its inception, were not those of a humble, self-effacing young man: "The present generation cannot appreciate the purity of my motives or the value of my exertions. I look to posterity for a good reputation. The unborn offspring of those who are now living will reverse the condemnatory decision of my contemporaries." Again, a few months later, he turned to a companion on leaving a meeting to remark, "You may someday write my biography."

Garrison was not averse to comparing himself to the Apostles, though he obviously possessed little of their patience and forbearance. He rarely forgot or forgave those who differed with him, and occasionally he took more credit where less was due without the slightest embarrassment. He had not, as Alcott put it trenchantly, "won those self-victories which lead to the superior powers of those who have won themselves." Significantly, Garrison had only a limited circle of close friends—"God's choreboy" Samuel May, [Oliver] Johnson, [Josiah] Quincy, and, closest of all, George Thompson, a man much like himself. Garrison lived in terms of his future epitaph, and carried his own Westminster Abbey about with him.

The Garrison Legend

William Lloyd Garrison's place in history was hotly debated in his own time. His admirers made him a greater man than he was, and his opponents gave him less praise than he deserved. According to Wendell Phillips, Garrison "began, inspired, and largely controlled" the entire abolition movement from beginning to end. Another idolator called him "lawgiver at Washington, inspirer of Presidential policy, and framer of the greatest war of modern times." But William Birney regarded Garrisonism as "the most utter abortion known in the history of this country," and Henry Ward Beecher characterized him as "no more than a blister" on the antislavery movement. Neither the Tappans [brothers Lewis and Arthur], nor Birney, nor Lundy, nor [Theodore Dwight] Weld, nor any of the pioneer abolitionists beyond New England thought of Garrison as more than an intractable, disturbing though sincere and devoted co-worker whose misguided zeal sometimes brought more harm than good to the cause.

The Garrison legend was partly the result of reams of uncritical praise poured out by Garrisonians—May, Johnson, Phillips, and others—in contrast to the comparative silence of those who opposed him. More than a little of Garrison's own conviction of immortality rubbed off on his followers. "Garrison has an army of men to write him up," said E.L. Pierce in 1892, "and his writers are unscrupulous." Those who admired Garrison gloried in praising him; those who opposed him charitably kept quiet.

It is only fair to grant Garrison pre-eminence in the first decade of abolition agitation. He personified its aggressive phase, publicized it for better or worse, and drove its issues deep into the national conscience. But he did not begin abolitionism, nor did he organize it. Weld and the Westerners, and the Tappans and the New Yorkers, deserve a large share of the credit; had Garrison never existed things might have been much the same. The movement, set in motion by others, was carried to its conclusion by methods he could not accept and ideas he could not understand. Abolition passed through him, not from him.

Yet Garrison was a person of real historical importance, for he was a symbol to his generation of the moral and ideological conflict that took its final shape in the Civil War. To the South, he represented all that was baleful and dangerous. Whatever his insistence on pacific intentions, he stirred up violent resentments and his appeals reached the passions rather than the consciences of slaveholders. His principle of "moral agitation" against slavery created only agitation. The proslavery forces, already consolidating, could concentrate all their fear and anger on him. If the approaching conflict was irrepressible, Garrison was at least a factor in convincing the South that it was so. By proslavery logic, Garrison led to John Brown; Brown led to Lincoln; Garrison, Brown, and Lincoln together led to an intolerable conclusion. It was easier for the South to argue from personalities rather than from principles, and Garrison was a personality no Southerner could overlook. By very little effort of his own he became a bogeyman to the South and a personification to it of things to come.

To the North, Garrison was a goad, a prick to the conscience, a symbol of the moral problem of slavery that remained unsolved despite compromises, conciliations, and tacit agreements to disregard it. Slavery, no matter how it was explained or rationalized, *did* exist; the fact of its existence *was* an anomaly in a nation dedicated to life, liberty, and the individual's right to pursue happiness. Garrison, more than any other one person, shattered the "conspiracy of silence." One might decry his invective, censure his methods, or deny his appeal to disorder; one could never shut out his clamor. To disagree with Garrison men had to face up to the problem, rethink their beliefs, examine their own consciences. When men did this, slavery was doomed. Garrison contributed relatively little to the philosophy of abolitionism. He had only a single thought—that "slavery was a crime, a damning crime"—but he made other men think, though he sometimes muddled their thinking. Economic and political events that Garrison neither knew nor cared about made slavery a national issue and precipitated the war. But it had its moral causes too, which Garrison's career aptly symbolized to the victorious North.

CHAPTER 4

Slavery Divides a Nation

 **Chapter Preface**

"Perhaps no decade in the history of the United States has been so filled with tense and crucial moments as the ten years leading to the Civil War, and closely connected with the majority of these crises was the problem of slavery," writes Robert William Fogel in his book *Without Consent or Contract: The Rise and Fall of American Slavery.* In the 1850s, the divisive debate over slavery came to a climax as it became entwined with a variety of different events and social forces.

The discovery of gold in California and the acquisition of new southwestern territories after the Mexican War in 1848 greatly spurred the westward movement. Slaveholding and abolitionist interests deadlocked over the question of whether slavery should be permitted in the new territories. The result was the Compromise of 1850, under which California was admitted as a free state; the question of whether to allow slavery in the territories of New Mexico, Nevada, Arizona, and Utah was deferred until they applied for statehood; and a tougher Fugitive Slave Law was passed. Southerners warned that they would remain in the Union only if the compromise was honored in the North. However, to the anger of Southerners, militant abolitionists rescued many Northern runaways that the new law mandated be sent back to slavery in the South.

The 1852 publication of *Uncle Tom's Cabin,* a popular novel that condemned slavery, further split the nation, and whatever semblance of harmony that still existed between North and South was all but destroyed by the 1854 Kansas-Nebraska Act, which allowed those territories to decide for themselves whether to allow slavery. In Kansas, the result was violence between pro- and antislavery factions that foreshadowed the Civil War. The antislavery Republican Party was formed, in large part as a response to the Kansas-Nebraska Act.

Proslavery forces won a short-term victory with the Supreme Court's 1857 decision in *Scott v. Sanford.* Dred Scott was a slave whose owner, a U.S. Army officer, had taken Scott to live in Illinois, a free state, and Wisconsin, a free territory, for a long period of time. When Scott's owner returned him to Missouri, a slave state, and then subsequently died, Scott sued for his freedom, claiming that he should be free because of the years he had lived on free soil. The case went to the Supreme Court, which ruled not only that Scott must remain a slave but also that all slaves and descendants of slaves were noncitizens and thus had no right to sue in federal court. The Supreme Court further ruled that Congress could not prohibit slavery in emerging territories.

With this clear-cut proslavery ruling from the nation's highest court, abolitionists became convinced that only drastic measures would bring an end to slavery. Southerners, in turn, were convinced that abolitionist zealots would stop at nothing in their attacks on the South.

These fears were partially validated by John Brown's 1859 raid on Harpers Ferry, Virginia (which is now in West Virginia). Brown was an ardent abolitionist who planned to establish a mountain stronghold where fugitive slaves could flee and from which he and his men could instigate slave insurrections. On October 16, 1859, he and roughly twenty followers took over the town of Harpers Ferry, seizing a federal arsenal of weapons stored there. They were soon captured by state and federal troops, but the incident had much of the South convinced that widespread, armed conflict with antislavery forces was imminent.

Ultimately, the event that prompted the first seven Southern states to secede from the Union was the 1860 election of Republican candidate Abraham Lincoln. Although many of his Northern supporters worried that Lincoln took too moderate a stance on abolition, the election of an openly antislavery candidate was, for the South, the last straw.

"It was the question of slavery . . . that brought the country to the impasse of 1860," writes Fogel. "It was in an atmosphere of slavery that the weapons for waging the Civil War were sharpened. It was the question of slavery that sundered the sections and forced them to settle the question by a bloody war." The specific questions about slavery that divided the country are explored in the following chapter.

Viewpoint 1

"I believe this government cannot endure permanently half slave *and half* free.*"*

Popular Sovereignty over Slavery Divides the Nation

Abraham Lincoln

Before becoming president, Abraham Lincoln served one term as a congressman from Illinois and in 1858 challenged incumbent Stephen A. Douglas for a seat in the U.S. Senate. Lincoln launched his election campaign with the June 16 speech reprinted below, in which he challenged Douglas on the issue of "popular sovereignty"—the idea that local settlers of the new territories should decide whether to legalize slavery or not. Douglas was a vocal supporter of popular sovereignty, while Lincoln felt that the decision to legalize or outlaw slavery had to be made on a national level.

Lincoln summarizes the recent developments in the slavery debate—notably the Compromise of 1850 and the 1854 Kansas-Nebraska Act, which supported the concept of popular sovereignty, and the 1857 Dred Scott decision, which invalidated previous congressional laws limiting slavery in the western territories. Lincoln argues that these developments are part of

Abraham Lincoln, speech before the Republican State Convention, Springfield, IL, June 16, 1858.

an ominous trend that, if continued, would make slavery legal throughout the United States.

Lincoln's speech eventually led to the famous Lincoln-Douglas debates concerning slavery. Douglas won the 1858 senatorial campaign, but the national prominence Lincoln achieved as a result of the debates played a key role in his 1860 election to the presidency.

*M*r. President, and Gentlemen of the Convention:
If we could first know where we are, and whither we are tending, we could better judge what to do, and how to do it. We are now far into the fifth year, since a policy was initiated with the avowed object, and confident promise, of putting an end to slavery agitation. Under the operation of that policy, that agitation has not only not ceased, but has constantly augmented. In my opinion, it will not cease, until a crisis shall have been reached and passed. "A house divided against itself cannot stand." I believe this government cannot endure permanently half slave and half free. I do not expect the Union to be dissolved—I do not expect the house to fall—but I do expect it will cease to be divided. It will become all one thing, or all the other. Either the opponents of slavery will arrest the further spread of it, and place it where the public mind shall rest in the belief that it is in the course of ultimate extinction; or its advocates will push it forward, till it shall become alike lawful in all the States, old as well as new—North as well as South.

Have we no tendency to the latter condition?

Let any one who doubts, carefully contemplate that now almost complete legal combination—piece of machinery, so to speak—compounded of the Nebraska doctrine, and the Dred Scott decision. Let him consider not only what work the machinery is adapted to do, and how well adapted; but also, let him study the history of its construction, and trace, if he can, or rather fail, if he can, to trace the evidences of design, and concert of action, among its chief architects, from the beginning.

The new year of 1854 found slavery excluded from more than half the States by State Constitutions, and from most of the national territory by Congressional prohibition. Four days later, commenced the struggle which ended in repealing that Congressional prohibition. This opened all the national territory to slavery, and was the first point gained.

But, so far, Congress only had acted; and an indorsement by the people, real or apparent, was indispensable, to save the point already gained, and give chance for more.

This necessity had not been overlooked; but had been provided for, as well as might be, in the notable argument of "squatter sovereignty," otherwise called "sacred right of self-government," which latter phrase, though expressive of the only rightful basis of any government, was so perverted in this attempted use of it as to amount to just this: That if any one man choose to enslave another, no third man shall be allowed to object. That argument was incorporated into the Nebraska bill itself, in the language which follows: "*It being the true intent and meaning of this act not to legislate slavery into any Territory or State, nor to exclude it therefrom; but to leave the people thereof perfectly free to form and regulate their domestic institutions in their own way, subject only to the Constitution of the United States.*" Then opened the roar of loose declamation in favor of "Squatter Sovereignty," and "sacred right of self-government." "But," said opposition members, "let us amend the bill so as to expressly declare that the people of the Territory may exclude slavery." "Not we," said the friends of the measure; and down they voted the amendment.

While the Nebraska bill was passing through Congress, a law case involving the question of a negro's freedom, by reason of his owner having voluntarily taken him first into a free State and then into a Territory covered by the Congressional prohibition, and held him as a slave for a long time in each, was passing through the U.S. Circuit Court for the District of Missouri; and both Nebraska bill and law suit were brought to a decision in the same month of May, 1854. The negro's name was "Dred Scott," which name now designates the decision finally made in the case. Before the then next Presidential election, the law case came to, and was argued in, the Supreme Court of the United States; but the decision of it was deferred until after the election. Still, before the election, Senator Trumbull, on the floor of the Senate, requested the leading advocate of the Nebraska bill to state his opinion whether the people of a Territory can constitutionally exclude slavery from their limits; and the latter answers: "That is a question for the Supreme Court."

The election came. Mr. [James] Buchanan was elected, and the indorsement, such as it was, secured. That was the second point gained. The indorsement, however, fell short of a clear popular majority by nearly four hundred thousand votes, and so, perhaps, was not overwhelmingly reliable and satisfactory. The outgoing President, in his last annual message, as impressively as possible echoed back upon the people the weight and authority of the indorsement. The Supreme Court met again; did not announce their decision, but ordered a re-argument. The Presidential inauguration came, and still no decision of the court; but the incoming President in his inaugural address, fervently exhorted the people to abide by the forthcoming decision, whatever it might be. Then, in a few days, came the decision.

The Dred Scott Decision

The reputed author [Stephen Douglas] of the Nebraska bill finds an early occasion to make a speech at this capital indorsing the Dred Scott decision, and vehemently denouncing all opposition to it. The new President, too, seizes the early occasion of the Silliman letter to indorse and strongly construe that decision, and to express his astonishment that any different view had ever been entertained!

At length a squabble springs up between the President and the author of the Nebraska bill, on the mere question of fact, whether the Lecompton Constitution was or was not, in any just sense, made by the people of Kansas; and in that quarrel the latter declares that all he wants is a fair vote for the people, and that he cares not whether slavery be voted down or voted up. I do not understand his declaration that he cares not whether slavery be voted down or voted up, to be intended by him other than as an apt definition of the policy he would impress upon the public mind— the principle for which he declares he has suffered so much, and is ready to suffer to the end. And well may he cling to that principle. If he has any parental feeling, well may he cling to it. That principle is the only shred left of his original Nebraska doctrine. Under the Dred Scott decision "squatter sovereignty" squatted out of existence, tumbled down like temporary scaffolding—like the mould at the foundry served through one blast and fell back into loose sand—helped to carry an election, and then was kicked to the winds. His late joint struggle with the Republicans, against the Lecompton Constitution, involves nothing of the original Nebraska doctrine. That struggle was made on a point—the right of a people to make their own constitution—upon which he and the Republicans have never differed.

Legal Machinery Supporting Slavery

The several points of the Dred Scott decision, in connection with Senator Douglas's "care not" policy, constitute the piece of machinery, in its present state of advancement. This was the third point gained. The working points of that machinery are:

First, That no negro slave, imported as such from Africa, and no descendant of such slave, can ever be a citizen of any State, in the sense of that term as used in the Constitution of the United States. This point is made in order to deprive the negro, in every possible event, of the benefit of that provision of the United States Constitution, which declares that "The citizens of each State shall be entitled to all privileges and immunities of citizens in the several States."

Secondly, That "subject to the Constitution of the United States," neither Congress nor a Territorial Legislature can exclude slavery from any United States territory. This point is made in order that individual men may fill up the Territories with slaves, without danger of losing them as property, and thus to enhance the chances of permanency to the institution through all the future.

Thirdly, That whether the holding a negro in actual slavery in a free State, makes him free, as against the holder, the United States courts will not decide, but will leave to be decided by the courts of any slave State the negro may be forced into by the master. This point is made, not to be pressed immediately, but, if acquiesced in for awhile, and apparently indorsed by the people at an election, then to sustain the logical conclusion that what Dred Scott's master might lawfully do with Dred Scott, in the free State of Illinois, every other master may lawfully do with any other one, or one thousand slaves, in Illinois, or in any other free State.

Auxiliary to all this, and working hand in hand with it, the Nebraska doctrine, or what is left of it, is to educate and mould public opinion, at least Northern public opinion, not to care whether slavery is voted down or voted up. This shows exactly where we now are; and partially, also, whither we are tending.

A Conspiracy?

It will throw additional light on the latter, to go back, and run the mind over the string of historical facts already stated. Several things will now appear less dark and mysterious than they did when they were transpiring. The people were to be left "perfectly free," "subject only to the Constitution." What the Constitution had to do with it, outsiders could not then see.

Plainly enough now, it was an exactly fitted niche, for the Dred Scott decision to afterward come in, and declare the perfect freedom of the people to be just no freedom at all. Why was the amendment, expressly declaring the right of the people, voted down? Plainly enough now: the adoption of it would have spoiled the niche for the Dred Scott decision. Why was the court decision held up? Why even a Senator's individual opinion withheld, till after the Presidential election? Plainly enough now: the speaking out then would have damaged the perfectly free argument upon which the election was to be carried. Why the outgoing President's felicitation on the indorsement? Why the delay of a reargument? Why the incoming President's advance exhortation in favor of the decision? These things look like the cautious patting and petting of a spirited horse, preparatory to mounting him, when it is dreaded that he may give the rider a fall. And why the hasty after indorsement of the decision by the President and others?

We cannot absolutely know that all these exact adaptations are the result of preconcert. But when we see a lot of framed timbers, different portions of which we know have been gotten out at different times and places and by different workmen—Stephen, Franklin, Roger and James, for instance—and when we see these timbers joined together, and see they exactly make the frame of a house or a mill, all the tenons and mortices exactly fitting, and all the lengths and proportions of the different pieces exactly adapted to their respective places, and not a piece too many or too few— not omitting even scaffolding—or, if a single piece be lacking, we see the place in the frame exactly fitted and prepared yet to bring such a piece in—in such a case, we find it impossible not to believe that Stephen and Franklin and Roger and James all understood one another from the beginning, and all worked upon a common plan or draft drawn up before the first blow was struck.

Viewpoint 2

"You must allow the people to decide for themselves whether [slavery] is a good or an evil."

Popular Sovereignty Should Decide Slavery

Stephen A. Douglas

Stephen A. Douglas was a U.S. senator from Illinois from 1846 to 1861 and was a candidate for president in 1860. He is perhaps best remembered for his debates with political rival Abraham Lincoln, whom he defeated in the 1858 Illinois senatorial campaign.

The following viewpoint is taken from a speech Douglas gave in Chicago on July 9, 1858, during his reelection campaign against Lincoln. The campaign featured debates between the two candidates over the issue of slavery, especially whether slavery should be allowed to expand in the western territories. Douglas favored "popular sovereignty"—that local communities of the territories themselves should decide whether to legalize slavery. This principle was central to the 1854 Kansas-Nebraska Act, a law Douglas sponsored, that permitted the slavery status of the Kansas and Nebraska territories to be decided by the local residents. In this speech, Douglas also defends the 1857 Dred Scott

Stephen A. Douglas, speech, Chicago, IL, July 9, 1858.

ruling, in which the Supreme Court ruled that blacks have no standing or rights under the U.S. Constitution.

Douglas defeated Lincoln in the 1858 senatorial election. Two years later, he received the Democratic Party's nomination for president, but was defeated by Lincoln, the candidate of the new Republican Party. Douglas subsequently worked in the Senate in support of Lincoln and the Union until his death in 1861.

I regard the great principle of popular sovereignty, as having been vindicated and made triumphant in this land, as a permanent rule of public policy in the organization of Territories and the admission of new States. Illinois took her position upon this principle many years ago. . . .

The People Must Decide

I deny the right of Congress to force a slaveholding State upon an unwilling people. I deny their right to force a free State upon an unwilling people. I deny their right to force a good thing upon a people who are unwilling to receive it. The great principle is the right of every community to judge and decide for itself, whether a thing is right or wrong, whether it would be good or evil for them to adopt it; and the right of free action, the right of free thought, the right of free judgment upon the question is dearer to every true American than any other under a free government. . . . It is no answer to this argument to say that slavery is an evil, and hence should not be tolerated. You must allow the people to decide for themselves whether it is a good or an evil. You allow them to decide for themselves whether they desire a Maine liquor law or not; you allow them to decide for themselves what kind of common schools they will have; what system of banking they will adopt, or whether they will adopt any at all; you allow them to decide for themselves the relations between husband and wife, parent and child, guardian and ward; in fact, you allow them to decide for themselves all other questions, and why not upon this question? Whenever you put a limitation upon the right of any people to decide what laws they want, you have destroyed the fundamental principle of self-government. . . .

Mr. Lincoln made a speech before that Republican Convention which unanimously nominated him for the Senate—a speech evidently well prepared and carefully written—in which he states the basis upon which he proposes to carry on the campaign during this summer. In it he lays down two distinct propositions which I shall notice, and upon which I shall take a direct and bold issue with him.

His first and main proposition I will give in his own language, scripture quotations and all [laughter]; I give his exact language—"'A house divided against itself cannot stand.' I believe this government cannot endure, permanently, half *slave* and half *free*. I do not expect the Union to be *dissolved*. I do not expect the house to *fall*; but I do expect it to cease to be divided. It will become *all* one thing or *all* the other."

In other words, Mr. Lincoln asserts, as a fundamental principle of this government, that there must be uniformity in the local laws and domestic institutions of each and all the States of the Union; and he therefore invites all the non-slaveholding States to band together, organize as one body, and make war upon slavery in Kentucky, upon slavery in Virginia, upon the Carolinas, upon slavery in all of the slaveholding States in this Union, and to persevere in that war until it shall be exterminated.

He then notifies the slaveholding States to stand together as a unit and make an aggressive war upon the free States of this Union with a view of establishing slavery in them all; of forcing it upon Illinois, of forcing it upon New York, upon New England, and upon every other free State, and that they shall keep up the warfare until it has been formally established in them all. In other words, Mr. Lincoln advocates boldly and clearly a war of sections, a war of the North against the South, of the free States against the slave States—a war of extermination—to be continued relentlessly until the one or the other shall be subdued, and all the States shall either become free or become slave.

Now, my friends, I must say to you frankly, that I take bold, unqualified issue with him upon that principle. I assert that it is neither desirable nor possible that there should be uniformity in the local institutions and domestic regulations of the different States of this Union. . . .

The framers of the Constitution well understood that each locality, having separate and distinct interests, required separate and distinct laws, domestic institutions, and police regulations adapted to its own wants and its own condition; and they acted on the presumption, also, that these laws and institutions would be as diversified and as dissimilar as the States would be numerous, and that no two would be precisely alike, because the interests of no two would be precisely the same. Hence, I assert, that the great fundamental principle which underlies our complex system of State and Federal Governments, contemplated diversity and dissimilarity in the local institutions and domestic affairs of each and every State then in the Union, or thereafter to be admitted into the Confederacy.

I therefore conceive that my friend, Mr. Lincoln, has totally misapprehended the great principles upon which our government rests. Uniformity in local and domestic affairs would be destructive of State rights, of State sovereignty, of personal liberty and personal freedom. Uniformity is the parent of despotism the world over, not only in politics, but in religion. Wherever the doctrine of uniformity is proclaimed, that all the States must be free or all slave, that all labor must be white or all black, that all the citizens of the different States must have the same privileges or be governed by the same regulations, you have destroyed the greatest safeguard which our institutions have thrown around the rights of the citizen.

How could this uniformity be accomplished, if it was desirable and possible? There is but one mode in which it could be obtained, and that must be by abolishing the State Legislatures, blotting out State sovereignty, merging the rights and sovereignty of the States in one consolidated empire, and vesting Congress with the plenary power to make all the police regulations, domestic and local laws, uniform throughout the limits of the Republic. When you shall have done this, you will have uniformity. Then the States will all be slave or all be free; then negroes will vote everywhere or nowhere; then you will have a Maine liquor law in every State or none; then you will have uniformity in all things, local and domestic, by the authority of the Federal Government. But when you attain that uniformity, you will have converted these thirty-two sovereign, independent States into one consolidated empire, with the uniformity of disposition reigning triumphant throughout the length and breadth of the land.

From this view of the case, my friends, I am driven irresistibly to the conclusion that diversity, dissimilarity, variety in all our local and domestic institutions, is the great safeguard of our liberties; and that the framers of our institutions were wise, sagacious, and patriotic, when they made this government a confederation of sovereign States, with a Legislature for each, and conferred upon each Legislature the power to make all local and domestic institutions to suit the people it represented, without interference from any other State or from the general Congress of the Union. If we expect to maintain our liberties, we must preserve the rights and sovereignty of the States; we must maintain and carry out that great principle of self-government incorporated in the compromise measures of 1850; indorsed by the Illinois Legislature in 1851; emphatically embodied and carried out in the Kansas-Nebraska bill, and vindicated this year by the refusal to bring Kansas into the Union with a Constitution distasteful to her people.

The Dred Scott Case

The other proposition discussed by Mr. Lincoln in his speech consists in a crusade against the Supreme Court of the United States on account of the Dred Scott decision. On this question, also, I desire to say to you unequivocally, that I take direct and distinct issue with him. I have no warfare to make on the Supreme Court of the United States, either on account of that or any other decision which they have pronounced from that bench. The Constitution of the United States has provided that the powers of government (and the Constitution of each State has the same provision) shall be divided into three departments—executive, legislative, and judicial. The right and the province of expounding the Constitution, and constructing the law, is vested in the judiciary established by the Constitution. As a lawyer, I feel at liberty to appear before the Court and controvert any principle of law while the question is pending before the tribunal; but when the decision is made, my private opinion, your opinion, all other opinions must yield to the majesty of that authoritative adjudication. . . .

Hence, I am opposed to this doctrine of Mr. Lincoln, by which he proposes to take an appeal from the decision of the Supreme Court of the United States, upon this high constitutional question, to a Republican caucus sitting in the country. Yes, or any other caucus or town meeting, whether it be Republican, American, or Democratic. I respect the decisions of that august tribunal; I shall always bow in deference to them. I am a law-abiding man. I will sustain the Constitution of my country as our fathers have made it. I will yield obedience to the laws, whether I like them or not, as I find them on the statute book. I will sustain the judicial tribunals and constituted authorities in all matters within the pale of their jurisdiction as defined by the Constitution.

But I am equally free to say that the reason assigned by Mr. Lincoln for resisting the decision of the Supreme Court in the Dred Scott case, does not in itself meet my approbation. He objects to it because that decision declared that a negro descended from African parents, who were brought here and sold as slaves, is not, and cannot be, a citizen of the United States. He says it is wrong, because it deprives the negro of the benefits of that clause of the Constitution which says that citizens of one State shall enjoy all the privileges and immunities of citizens of the several States; in other words, he thinks it wrong because it deprives the negro of the privileges, immunities and rights of citizenship, which pertain, according to that decision, only to the white man.

I am free to say to you that in my opinion this government of ours is founded on the white basis. It was made by the white man, for the benefit of the white man, to be administered by white men, in such manner as they should determine. It is also true that a negro, an Indian, or any other man of inferior race to a white man, should be permitted to enjoy, and humanity requires that he should have all the rights, privileges and immunities which he is capable of exercising consistent with the safety of society. I would give him every right and every privilege which his capacity would enable him to enjoy, consistent with the good of the society in which he lived.

But you may ask me, what are these rights and these privileges? My answer is, that each State must decide for itself the nature and extent of these rights.

Illinois has decided for herself. We have decided that the negro shall not be a slave, and we have at the same time decided that he shall not vote, or serve on juries, or enjoy political privileges. I am content with that system of policy which we have adopted for ourselves. I deny the right of any other State to complain of our policy in that respect, or to interfere with it, or to attempt to change it. On the other hand, the State of Maine has decided that in that State a negro man may vote on an equality with the white man. The sovereign power of Maine had the right to prescribe that rule for herself. Illinois has no right to complain of Maine for conferring the right of negro suffrage, nor has Maine any right to interfere with, or complain of Illinois because she has denied negro suffrage. . . .

Thus you see, my fellow-citizens, that the issues between Mr. Lincoln and myself, as respective candidates for the U.S. Senate, as made up, are direct, unequivocal, and irreconcilable. He goes for uniformity in our domestic institutions, for a war of sections, until one or the other shall be subdued. I go for the great principle of the Kansas-Nebraska bill, the right of the people to decide for themselves.

Viewpoint 3

"The Union cause has suffered and is now suffering immensely from mistaken deference to Rebel slavery."

Freeing the Slaves Should Be the Primary War Aim

Horace Greeley

Horace Greeley founded the influential *New York Tribune* in 1841 and edited it for more than thirty years. Through his newspaper Greeley became an influential voice in national politics. He supported the antislavery cause and was an early member of the Republican Party. In 1872 he unsuccessfully ran for president.

The following viewpoint is taken from an open letter from Greeley to President Abraham Lincoln published in the August 19, 1862, edition of the *Tribune*. Lincoln had resisted abolitionists' calls for emancipation, believing it would hurt the Union cause by alienating slaveholding individuals and states that supported the Union. Greeley argues that the president should place a higher priority on freeing the slaves, and accuses Lincoln of being timid in dealing with the issue. He urges Lincoln to actively enforce the Confiscation Act, an 1862 law passed by Congress that called on the president to confiscate captured Confederate property, including slaves, and to put that property to use in the war effort.

Horace Greeley, "The Prayer of Twenty Million," *New York Tribune*, August 19, 1862.

*D*ear Sir:
I do not intrude to tell you—for you must know already—that a great proportion of those who triumphed in your election, and of all who desire the unqualified suppression of the rebellion now desolating our country, are sorely disappointed and deeply pained by the policy you seem to be pursuing with regard to the slaves of Rebels. I write only to set succinctly and unmistakably before you what we require, what we think we have a right to expect, and of what we complain.

I. We require of you, as the first servant of the republic, charged especially and pre-eminently with this duty, that you EXECUTE THE LAWS. Most emphatically do we demand that such laws as have been recently enacted, which therefore may fairly be presumed to embody the public will and to be dictated by the *present* needs of the republic, and which, after due consideration, have received your personal sanction, shall by you be carried into full effect and that you publicly and decisively instruct your subordinates that such laws exist, that they are binding on all functionaries and citizens, and that they are to be obeyed to the letter.

II. We think you are strangely and disastrously remiss in the discharge of your official and imperative duty with regard to the emancipating provisions of the new Confiscation Act. Those provisions were designed to fight slavery with liberty. They prescribe that men loyal to the Union, and willing to shed their blood in her behalf, shall no longer be held, with the nation's consent, in bondage to persistent, malignant traitors, who for twenty years have been plotting and for sixteen months have been fighting to divide and destroy our country. Why these traitors should be treated with tenderness by you, to the prejudice of the dearest rights of loyal men, we cannot conceive.

Slavery the Cause of Treason

III. We think you are unduly influenced by the councils, the representations, the menaces, of certain fossil politicians hailing from the border Slave states. Knowing well that the heartily, unconditionally loyal portion of the white citizens of those states do not expect nor desire that slavery shall be upheld to the prejudice of the Union—for the truth of which we appeal not only to every Re-

publican residing in those states but to such eminent loyalists as
H. Winter Davis, Parson Brownlow, the Union Central Committee of Baltimore, and to the *Nashville Union*—we ask you to consider that slavery is everywhere the inciting cause and sustaining
base of treason: the most slaveholding sections of Maryland and
Delaware being this day, though under the Union flag, in full sympathy with the rebellion, while the free labor portions of Tennessee and of Texas, though writhing under the bloody heel of
treason, are unconquerably loyal to the Union. . . .

It seems to us the most obvious truth that whatever strengthens
or fortifies slavery in the border states strengthens also treason and
drives home the wedge intended to divide the Union. Had you,
from the first, refused to recognize in those states, as here, any
other than unconditional loyalty—that which stands for the
Union, whatever may become of slavery—those states would have
been, and would be, far more helpful and less troublesome to the
defenders of the Union than they have been, or now are.

No Time for Timidity

IV. We think timid counsels in such a crisis calculated to prove
perilous, and probably disastrous. It is the duty of a government
so wantonly, wickedly assailed by rebellion as ours has been to op-
pose force to force in a defiant, dauntless spirit. It cannot afford
to temporize with traitors, nor with semi-traitors. . . .

V. We complain that the Union cause has suffered and is now
suffering immensely from mistaken deference to Rebel slavery.
Had you, sir, in your inaugural address, unmistakably given notice that in case the rebellion already commenced were persisted
in and your efforts to preserve the Union and enforce the laws
should be resisted by armed force, *you would recognize no loyal
person as rightfully held in slavery by a traitor*, we believe the rebellion would therein have received a staggering if not fatal blow.
At that moment, according to the returns of the most recent elec-
tions, the Unionists were a large majority of the voters of the Slave
states. But they were composed in good part of the aged, the feeble, the wealthy, the timid—the young, the reckless, the aspiring,
the adventurous had already been largely lured by the gamblers
and Negro traders, the politicians by trade and the conspirators

by instinct, into the toils of treason. Had you then proclaimed that rebellion would strike the shackles from the slaves of every traitor, the wealthy and the cautious would have been supplied with a powerful inducement to remain loyal. . . .

VI. We complain that the Confiscation Act which you approved is habitually disregarded by your generals, and that no word of rebuke for them from you has yet reached the public ear. Fremont's Proclamation and Hunter's Order favoring emancipation were promptly annulled by you; while Halleck's Number Three, forbidding fugitives from slavery to Rebels to come within his lines—an order as unmilitary as inhuman, and which received the hearty approbation of every traitor in America—with scores of like tendency, have never provoked even your remonstrance.

Refusing to Welcome Slaves

We complain that the officers of your armies have habitually repelled rather than invited the approach of slaves who would have gladly taken the risks of escaping from their Rebel masters to our camps, bringing intelligence often of inestimable value to the Union cause. We complain that those who *have* thus escaped to us, avowing a willingness to do for us whatever might be required, have been brutally and madly repulsed, and often surrendered to be scourged, maimed, and tortured by the ruffian traitors who pretend to own them. We complain that a large proportion of our regular Army officers, with many of the volunteers, evince far more solicitude to uphold slavery than to put down the rebellion.

And, finally, we complain that you, Mr. President, elected as a Republican, knowing well what an abomination slavery is and how emphatically it is the core and essence of this atrocious rebellion, seem never to interfere with these atrocities and never give a direction to your military subordinates, which does not appear to have been conceived in the interest of slavery rather than of freedom. . . .

VIII. On the face of this wide earth, Mr. President, there is not one disinterested, determined, intelligent champion of the Union cause who does not feel that all attempts to put down the rebellion and at the same time uphold its inciting cause are preposterous and futile; that the rebellion, if crushed out tomorrow, would be renewed within a year if slavery were left in full vigor; that Army officers who remain to this day devoted to slavery can at best be but halfway loyal to the Union; and that every hour of deference to slavery is an hour of added and deepened peril to the Union. I appeal to the testimony of your ambassadors in Europe. It is freely at your service, not at mine. Ask them to tell you candidly whether the seeming subserviency of your policy to the slaveholding, slavery-upholding interest is not the perplexity, the despair of statesmen of all parties, and be admonished by the general answer!

IX. I close as I began with the statement that what an immense majority of the loyal millions of your countrymen require of you is a frank, declared, unqualified, ungrudging execution of the laws of the land, more especially of the Confiscation Act. That act gives freedom to the slaves of Rebels coming within our lines, or whom those lines may at any time enclose—we ask you to render it due obedience by publicly requiring all your subordinates to recognize and obey it. The Rebels are everywhere using the late anti-Negro riots in the North, as they have long used your officers' treatment of Negroes in the South, to convince the slaves that they have nothing to hope from a Union success, that we mean in that case to sell them into a bitter bondage to defray the cost of the war.

Let them impress this as a truth on the great mass of their ignorant and credulous bondmen, and the Union will never be restored—never. We cannot conquer 10 million people united in solid phalanx against us, powerfully aided by Northern sympathizers and European allies. We must have scouts, guides, spies, cooks, teamsters, diggers, and choppers from the blacks of the South, whether we allow them to fight for us or not, or we shall be baffled and repelled.

As one of the millions who would gladly have avoided this struggle at any sacrifice but that of principle and honor, but who now feel that the triumph of the Union is indispensable, not only to the existence of our country but to the well-being of mankind, I entreat you to render a hearty and unequivocal obedience to the law of the land.

Viewpoint 4

"My paramount object in this struggle is to save the Union, and is not either to save or destroy slavery."

Preserving the Union Should Be the Primary War Aim

Abraham Lincoln

Abraham Lincoln was the president of the United States from 1861 to his assassination in 1865. His presidency was dominated by the Civil War: One month after he was elected, seven Southern states attempted to secede from the United States (they were later joined by four others), in large part to preserve the institution of slavery. As president, Lincoln was determined to preserve the Union. This focus was continually challenged by abolitionists who considered him too mild on the subject of slavery, and by those who sought to end the Civil War by accepting an independent Confederacy.

Lincoln was personally opposed to slavery and earlier in his career had favored gradual, compensated emancipation. But as president he hesitated to abolish slavery outright, believing that preserving the Union should take the highest priority. Lincoln succinctly expressed his views in the following August 22, 1862, letter, which the president wrote in reply to Horace Greeley's criticism of his policies.

Abraham Lincoln, "Letter to Horace Greeley," *New York Tribune*, August 22, 1862.

*D*ear Sir:
I have just read yours of the 19th, addressed to myself through the *New York Tribune*. If there be in it any statements or assumptions of fact which I may know to be erroneous, I do not now and here controvert them. If there be in it any inferences which I may believe to be falsely drawn, I do not now and here argue against them. If there be perceptible in it an impatient and dictatorial tone, I waive it in deference to an old friend, whose heart I have always supposed to be right.

As to the policy I "seem to be pursuing," as you say, I have not meant to leave anyone in doubt.

The Union Must Be Saved

I would save the Union. I would save it the shortest way under the Constitution. The sooner the national authority can be restored, the nearer the Union will be "the Union as it was." If there be those who would not save the Union unless they could at the same time *save* slavery, I do not agree with them. If there be those who would not save the Union unless they could at the same time *destroy* slavery, I do not agree with them. My paramount object in this struggle *is* to save the Union, and is *not* either to save or destroy slavery. If I could save the Union without freeing *any* slave, I would do it; and if I could save it by freeing *all* the slaves, I would do it; and if I could do it by freeing some and leaving others alone, I would also do that.

What I do about slavery and the colored race I do because I believe it helps to save this Union; and what I forbear I forbear because I do *not* believe it would help to save the Union. I shall do *less* whenever I shall believe what I am doing hurts the cause, and I shall do *more* whenever I shall believe doing more will help the cause. I shall try to correct errors when shown to be errors; and I shall adopt new views so fast as they shall appear to be true views.

I have here stated my purpose according to my view of *official* duty, and I intend no modification of my oft-expressed *personal* wish that all men, everywhere, could be free.

Viewpoint 5

"The peculiar institution's final destruction within an independent cotton South was inevitable."

Slavery Would Have Been Abolished Without the Civil War

Jeffrey Rogers Hummel

A question that is still debated by historians is whether America could have ended slavery without the violent and costly Civil War. Jeffrey Rogers Hummel, an economics and history professor at Golden State University in San Francisco, suggests that American slavery could have been ended by other means. Citing the experiences of the British West Indies and Brazil, where slavery was abolished without war, Hummel argues that President Abraham Lincoln could have let Southern states peaceably secede in 1861 and still have laid the groundwork for slavery's eventual demise. An independent Confederacy that shared a long border with the free United States would have found it highly difficult to prevent slaves from running away or rebelling.

Jeffrey Rogers Hummel, *Emancipating Slaves, Enslaving Free Men: A History of the American Civil War*. Chicago: Open Court Publishing Company, 1996. Copyright © 1996 by Jeffrey Rogers Hummel. Reproduced by permission.

As an excuse for civil war, maintaining the State's territorial integrity is bankrupt and reprehensible. Slavery's elimination is the only morally worthy justification. The fact that abolition was an unintended consequence in no way gainsays [denies] the accomplishment. "The nineteenth century was preeminently the century of emancipations," explains [historian] C. Vann Woodward. Small-scale emancipations began in the northern states during the previous century, and chattel slavery was not ended in coastal Kenya until 1907. But starting with the British colonies in 1833 and finishing with Brazil in 1888, over six million slaves achieved some kind of freedom in the Western Hemisphere. Four million were blacks in the United States. "The emancipation experience of the South," Woodward concludes, "dwarfs all others in scale and magnitude."

Yet this justification holds only if war was indeed necessary. No abolition was completely peaceful, but the United States and Haiti are just two among twenty-odd slave societies where violence predominated. The fact that emancipation overwhelmed such entrenched plantation economies as Cuba and Brazil suggests that slavery was politically moribund anyway. An ideological movement that had its meager roots in the eighteenth century eventually eliminated everywhere a labor system that had been ubiquitous throughout world civilizations for millennia. Historical speculations about an independent Confederacy halting or reversing this overwhelming momentum are hard to credit.

Lincoln's Options

When Lincoln took the presidential oath in 1861, letting the lower South secede in peace was a viable antislavery option. At the moment of Lincoln's inauguration the Union still retained more slave states than had left. Radical abolitionism, such as William Lloyd Garrison, had traditionally advocated northern secession from the South. They felt that this best hastened the destruction of slavery by allowing the free states to get out from under the Constitution's fugitive slave provision. Passionately opposing slavery and simultaneously favoring secession are therefore quite consistent. Yet hardly any modern account of the Union's fiery conflagration even acknowledges this untried alternative.

Revisionist Civil War historians at one time argued that slavery was *economically* doomed. Economists have subjected that claim to searching scrutiny, discovering in fact that American slavery was profitable and expanding. But as [historian] Eric Foner has perceptively noted, "plantation slavery had always been both a political and economic institution. It could not have existed without a host of legal and coercive measures designed to define the status of the black laborer and prevent the emergence of competing modes of social organization." In the United States these measures included restrictions on manumission [emancipation], disabilities against free blacks, compulsory slave patrols, and above all fugitive slave laws.

Slavery was doomed *politically* even if Lincoln had permitted the small Gulf Coast Confederacy[1] to depart in peace. The Republican-controlled Congress would have been able to work toward emancipation within the border states, where slavery was already declining. In due course the Radicals[2] could have repealed the Fugitive Slave Law of 1850. With chattels fleeing across the border and raising slavery's enforcement costs, the peculiar institution's final destruction within an independent cotton South was inevitable.

Even future Confederate Vice-President Alexander Stephens had judged "slavery much more secure in the Union than out of it." Secession was a gamble of pure desperation for slaveholders, only attempted because the institution clearly had no political future within the Union. The individual runaway both helped provoke secession—northern resistance to fugitive recapture being a major southern grievance—and ensured that secession would be unable to shield slavery in the end. Back in 1842, Joseph Rogers Underwood, representing Kentucky in the House of Representatives, warned his fellow Southerners that "the dissolution of the Union was the dissolution of slavery." Why? "Just as soon as Mason and Dixon's line and the Ohio river become the boundary between independent nations, slavery ceases in all the

1. the seven states that seceded prior to the outbreak of hostilities in Fort Sumter: South Carolina, Georgia, Louisiana, Mississippi, Florida, Alabama, and Texas
2. Republicans in Congress who strongly opposed slavery and supported black civil rights

border states. How could we retain our slaves, when they, in one hour, one day, or a week at furthest, could pass the boundary?" Once across, the slave could "then turn round and curse his master from the other shore." Nor would the peculiar institution's collapse stop at the border states. "Do you not see that sooner or later, this process would extend itself farther and farther south, rendering slave labor so precarious and uncertain that it could not be depended upon; and consequently a slave would become almost worthless; and thus the institution itself would gradually, but certainly, perish?"

Overthrow of Slavery in Brazil

Just such a process later accelerated the demise of slavery in Brazil. This slave economy was in 1825 the New World's second largest, holding in bondage only slightly fewer than the American South. Yet even before Brazil's abolition, manumission caused free blacks to exceed slaves in total numbers, with an estimated half those manumissions through self-purchase. By 1850 free blacks were 43 percent of the population, making a large constituency opposed to slavery. Although the government instituted gradual emancipation in 1871, the law freed only slaves born after its enactment, and only when they reached the age of twenty-one. Brazil also established a tax fund to purchase the freedom of those to whom the law did not apply, but during its operation three times as many purchased their own freedom or were granted manumission.

Brazilian abolitionists meanwhile succeeded in outlawing slavery in the northeastern state of Ceará in 1884. An underground railroad immediately came into existence. Planters retaliated with a fugitive slave law, but the law was widely evaded. The state of Amazonas and many cities joined Ceará. Slavery rapidly disintegrated in the coffee growing region of São Paulo. The value of slaves fell by 80 percent despite the fact that none was slated to be liberated through gradual emancipation. Finally in 1888 the government accepted a *fait accompli* and decreed immediate and uncompensated emancipation. The total number of slaves had already declined from two and a half million, or 30 percent of the population in 1850, to half a million, or less than 3 percent.

"Slavery could not last if the slaves had freedom within arm's length," recalled American abolitionist Moncure Conway. Slavery in the Cape Colony of southern Africa, for instance, depended upon the transportation of blacks from Mozambique and Madagascar and of east Indians. The so-called Hottentots [Khoisan people], indigenous to the area, were nearly impossible to keep enslaved because they could escape too easily. Civil War runaways so weakened the peculiar institution that the Confederacy itself turned toward emancipating and arming blacks. Slavery thus neither explains nor justifies Northern suppression of secession. The Union war effort reduces, in the words of Conway, to "mere manslaughter."

Comparing Civil War with Slave Insurrection

Brazilian abolitionists had also encouraged resistance by distributing arms to the slaves. An independent Confederacy still faced the specter of John Brown, who merely wished to bring the revolutionary right of secession down to the plantation. The massive uprising that Brown, Lysander Spooner, and David Walker each hoped for[3] would obviously have resulted in much loss of life, but worth speculation is whether it could ever have approached the Civil War's unmatched toll: one dead soldier for every six freed slaves. The war took nearly as many lives as the total number of slaves liberated without bloodshed in the British West Indies. Those who complacently accept this as a necessary sacrifice for eliminating an evil institution inexplicably blanch at the potential carnage of slave revolts.

Violence ultimately ended slavery, but violence of a very different nature. Rather than revolutionary violence wielded by bondsmen themselves from the bottom up, a violence that at least had the potential to be pinpointed against the South's minority of guilty slaveowners, the Civil War involved indiscriminate State violence directed from the top down. Nor would an insurgency's economic devastation likely have reached the war's $6.6 billion cost (in 1860

3. Abolitionist Brown led an abortive slave uprising in Virginia in 1859. Spooner, a white Boston abolitionist, published plans to incite and assist slave uprisings in the 1850s. Walker was a free black who wrote a pamphlet in 1828 calling for black revolution.

prices), about evenly divided between the two sides. The North's portion alone was enough to buy all slaves and set up each family with forty acres and a mule. John Brown's plan had the added advantage of actively mobilizing blacks in their own liberation. The social institutions that the revolutionaries would have ineluctably created could have altered the subsequent history of the southern race relations. On what consistent grounds can anyone find war between two governments morally superior to slave rebellion?

Viewpoint 6

"Peaceful secession . . . would not only have indefinitely delayed the freeing of U.S. slaves but would have thwarted the antislavery movement everywhere else in the world."

Slavery Would Have Continued Indefinitely Without the Civil War

Robert William Fogel

Robert William Fogel is director of the Center for Population Economics at the University of Chicago and the author of several books, including *Without Consent or Contract: The Rise and Fall of American Slavery*, from which the following viewpoint is excerpted. Fogel responds to the idea, first proposed by historian David M. Potter, that slavery could have been ended without the bloodshed of the Civil War. Fogel argues that the peaceful abolition of slavery was impossible as the Civil War began. He further maintains that the defeat of the Confederacy and the end of slavery in the United States had global ramifications that greatly strengthened the antislavery movement and other struggles for human rights worldwide. If the Confederacy had been allowed to establish itself peacefully, Fogel posits, slavery would have continued indefinitely and would likely have expanded.

For more than a century historians have been engaged in an intense debate about the causes of the Civil War. Although some scholars have held that slavery was *the* cause, others have developed complex analyses that draw distinctions between immediate and ultimate causes and that explore a variety of ways other than war that could have settled or at least contained the issue of slavery. They have also analyzed a wide range of economic, political, and cultural issues between the sections other than slavery that promoted antagonisms and that rival slavery (some believe they dominate it) as an explanation for the war. Among the most nagging of the moral questions to emerge from these debates is the one posed by David M. Potter, who, until his death in 1971, was one of the most respected historians of his generation.

In totaling up the balance sheet of the Civil War, Potter concluded: "Slavery was dead; secession was dead; and six hundred thousand men were dead." So one soldier died for six slaves who were freed and for ten white Southerners who were kept in the Union. In the face of so bloody a war, a "person is entitled to wonder," said Potter, "whether the Southerners could have been held and the slaves could not have been freed at a smaller per-capita cost." When he posed this problem it was still widely believed that slavery was an economically moribund system and the proposition that economic forces would eventually have solved the problem of slavery was tenable. Even so, there was a question of how soon. And if not, there was a question of when, if ever, southern slaveholders would have peacefully acceded to any scheme for emancipation, no matter how gradual, no matter how full the proffered compensation.

Prospects for Peaceful Abolition

Whatever the opportunity for a peaceful abolition of slavery along British lines before 1845, it surely was nonexistent after that date. To southern slaveholders, West Indian emancipation was a complete failure. It provided undeniable proof, if any was needed, of the malevolent designs that the abolitionists and their allies harbored for their class. They could plainly see that the economy of the West Indies was in shambles, that the personal fortunes of the West Indian planters had collapsed, and that the assurances made to these planters in 1833 to obtain their acquiescence to compensated emancipation were violated as soon as the planters were reduced to political impotency. Given such an assessment of the consequences of compensated emancipation, a peaceful end to slavery could only have been achieved if economic forces made slaves worthless or, more compelling, an absolute drain on the income of their owners.

From the mid-1840s on, however, the slave economy of the South was vigorous and growing rapidly. Whatever the pessimism of masters during the economic crises of 1826–1831 and 1840–1845, during the last half of the 1840s and most of the 1850s they foresaw a continuation of their prosperity and, save for the political threat from the North, numerous opportunities for its expansion. The main thrust of cliometric research has demonstrated that this economic optimism was well-founded; it has also undermined the competing thesis that slavery was gradually expiring of its own internal economic contradictions. Although he presented it in a political rather than an economic context, [historian Kenneth] Stampp's rejoinder to Potter is equally germane here. A "person is also entitled to ask," he said, "how many more generations of black men should have been forced to endure life in bondage in order to avoid its costly and violent end."

After the [1860] election of Lincoln the choices open to northern foes of slavery no longer included the moderate strategy—which was to restrict and gradually undermine the slave economy as the British abolitionists had done between 1812 and 1833, and as the Brazilian abolitionists were able to do in the 1880s. Once the cotton states of the South moved on to the secessionist path, peaceful restoration of the Union was no longer possible merely by returning to the status quo of c. 1850, even if the rights of slaveholders everywhere below 36° 30' and of their property rights in fugitives were embodied in new, irrevocable amendments to the Constitution, as was proposed in the Crittenden Resolutions. The majority of the Senate and House members from these states rejected all such compromises. They were convinced that northern hostility to slavery precluded a union that would promote the economic, political, and international objectives that had become predominant among politicians of the cotton South. As the votes for the delegates to the state convention indicated, by early 1861 majority opinion in the deep South held that a future in the Union "promised nothing but increasingly galling economic exploitation by the dominant section and the rapid reduction of the South to political impotence."

So the central moral problem of the Civil War is not the one posed by Potter but the one posed in Stampp's response to him. By early 1861 maintenance of peace required not merely northern acquiescence to the status quo of c. 1850, but acquiescence to the existence of an independent confederacy dedicated to the promotion of slavery. It follows that assessment of the dilemma posed by Stampp requires more than weighing the sin of slavery against the sin of war. It requires also a consideration of the likely chain of events that would have unfolded if the South had been unshackled from northern restraint and allowed to become a worldwide champion of slavery and of aristocratic republicanism.

What Would Have Happened?

Consideration of what might have happened if the Confederate states had been allowed to secede peacefully is an excursion into beliefs about a world that never existed. Even if these beliefs are based on patterns of behavior during the years leading up to the war, patterns of behavior that provide a reasonable basis for prediction, the best predictions are necessarily shrouded in uncertainty and open to debate. Yet there is no way of dealing with the moral issues of the Civil War that avoids these "counterfactual propositions" (as philosophers call them). Every historian who has set out to deal with the causes of the Civil War (certainly all those who have debated its necessity or avoidability) has implicitly or explicitly presumed what would have happened to slavery if some events had unfolded in a way that was different from the actual course. Indeed, much of the voluminous literature on the causes of the Civil War is nothing more or less than a marshaling of evidence on the events leading up to the Civil War that is dictated by different visions of this counterfactual world.

Peaceful secession, I believe, would not only have indefinitely delayed the freeing of U.S. slaves but would have thwarted the antislavery movement everywhere else in the world. It would also very likely have slowed down the struggle to extend suffrage and other democratic rights to the lower classes in Europe, and it might have eroded whatever rights had already been granted to them in both Europe and North America. Since the forces of reaction everywhere would have been greatly encouraged, and those of democracy and reform demoralized, it is likely that the momentum for liberal reform would have been replaced by a drive for aristocratic privilege under the flags of paternalism and the preservation of order.

Such a vision of events may seem fantastic to those accustomed to the rhetoric and conventions of modern (plebeian) democracy. We live in a world in which the underprivileged regularly contend for power: abroad, through labor and socialist parties; at home, through such influential organizations as the AFL-CIO, NOW, and the Rainbow Coalition. However, during the 1850s and 1860s democracy as we now know it, and lower-class rights generally, hung in the balance throughout the Western world. In Great Britain the great majority of workers were disfranchised, trade unions were illegal, strikes were criminal acts, and quitting a job without an employer's permission was a breach of contract punishable by stiff fines and years of imprisonment. The legacy of serfdom was heavy in Portugal, Spain, Italy, eastern Prussia, Russia, Hungary, the Balkans, Turkey, and much of South America, while slavery flourished in Cuba, Brazil, Surinam, Africa, the Middle East, and numerous other places. Even in the North, strikes were proscribed, property qualifications for voting were widespread until the 1820s (and were still enforced against free blacks in New York and other states in the 1860s), and vagrancy laws were a powerful club against workers. The movement for the disfranchisement of the foreign born was partially successful in some northern states during the 1850s, and in Virginia a referendum to reinstate a property qualification for voters was approved on the eve of the Civil War.

The fact that the liberals who dominated politics in the North and in Britain rejected slavery as a solution to the menace posed by an unconstrained lower-class "rabble" does not mean that they were oblivious to the menace. Reformers such as Lord [Thomas B.] Macaulay remained adamant in the opinion that the franchise had to be restricted to men of property and that a large police force and army were needed to keep the lower classes in check. Even such a celebrated champion of the propertyless masses as Horace Greeley supported the use of military force to put down strikes.

The Revisionists' View of the Civil War

In the first decades after it ended, the Civil War was widely thought of as an "irrepressible conflict," an unfortunate but inevitable war caused by generations of division between North and South not just over slavery, but also over many other issues of economics, politics, and culture. Beginning around the 1930s, a new school of though emerged. The Civil War "revisionists," led by historian Avery Craven, held that the war was not unavoidable, that differences between North and South were not so great, and that blame for the Civil War lay with extremists in both the North and South.

In his book The Imperiled Union, *historian Kenneth M. Stampp offers a critical view of revisionist arguments that the Civil War should not have been fought. In the excerpt below, Stampp focuses on how revisionists have approached the question of whether the number of slaves freed after the Civil War justifies the number of lives lost in the conflict.*

Historians do sometimes indulge in "counterfactual history"—informed speculation about how things would have been if certain other things had or had not happened—and that essentially is the kind of history that revisionists have written. They were interested not only in explaining why the Civil War occurred but in showing how, by a different course of action, it could have been avoided and how much better off the country would have been if its history had been one of continued peace. . . .

Potential Power of the Confederacy

If the Confederacy had been allowed to establish itself peacefully, to work out economic and diplomatic policies, and to develop international alliances, it would have emerged as a major international power. Although its population was relatively small, its great wealth would have made it a force to be reckoned with. The Confederacy would probably have used its wealth and military power to establish itself as the dominant nation in Latin America, perhaps annexing Cuba and Puerto Rico, Yucatan, and Nicaragua as

Their conviction that evolutionary forces would soon have ended slavery peacefully was a basic premise of their case. . . .

[Historian] E. Merton Coulter made the point concisely: "The Civil War was not worth the cost. . . . What good the war produced would have come with time in an orderly way; the bad would not have come at all."

Precisely when slavery's peaceful end would have come no revisionist could say, but most of them guessed that it could have lasted no longer than another generation, or no later than the end of the nineteenth century. In any event, when emancipation came, it would not have cost the life of one soldier for every six slaves freed—a per capita cost that [David M.] Potter quite understandably found rather staggering. On the other hand, the postponement of emancipation for a generation, while saving the lives of soldiers, would have exacted its own price. It would have meant that the four million slaves of 1860, as well as their descendants, would have remained in bondage until the forces anticipated by the revisionists moved white masters in their own good time to grant freedom to their black laborers. How to balance the lives of half a million soldiers against the prolonged bondage of four million slaves is a question with profound moral implications; how one resolves it will doubtless depend in part on one's judgment of slavery itself.

Kenneth M. Stampp, *The Imperiled Union: Essays on the Background of the Civil War*. New York: Oxford University Press, 1980.

well as countering Britain's antislavery pressures on Brazil. Whether the Confederacy would have sought to counter British antislavery policies in Africa or to form alliances with the principal slave-trading nations of the Middle East is more uncertain, but these would have been options.

The Confederacy could have financed its expansionist, proslavery policies by exploiting the southern monopoly of cotton production. A 5¢ sales tax on cotton not only would have put most of the burden of such policies on foreign consumers, but would have yielded about $100 million annually during the 1860s—50 percent more than the entire federal budget on the eve of the Civil War. With such a revenue the Confederacy could have emerged as one of the world's strongest military powers, maintaining a standing army several times as large as the North's, rapidly developing a major navy, and conducting an aggressive foreign policy. Such revenues would also have permitted it to covertly or overtly finance aristocratic forces in Europe who were vying with democratic ones for power across the Continent.

Shrewd manipulation of its monopoly of raw cotton would have permitted the Confederacy to reward its international friends and punish its enemies. Embargoes or other restrictions on the sale of raw cotton could have delivered punishing blows to the economies of England and the Northeast, where close to 20 percent of the nonagricultural labor force was directly or indirectly engaged in the manufacture and sale of cotton textiles. The resulting unemployment and losses of wealth would have disrupted both the labor and capital markets in these regions, and probably speeded up the emergence of a large textile industry in the South. The West would also have been destabilized economically, since the decline of the Northeast would have severely contracted the market for western agricultural products. As the Confederacy shifted more of its labor into manufacturing, trade, and the military, it would probably have developed an increasing deficit in food, making it again a major market for the grain, dairy, and meat surpluses of the Northwest.

Such economic developments would have generated strong political pressures in the North for a modus vivendi with the Confederacy. Northern politics would have been further complicated by any border states, such as Maryland, Kentucky, and Missouri, that might have remained inside the Union. Attempts to appropriate their slave property would have run a high risk of further secessions. The Republicans not only would have borne the responsibility for the economic crisis created by the rise of the Confederacy, but would have lost the plank on which the party had risen to power. With the bulk of slaveowners prohibited from entry into northern territories because of secession, the claim that the victory by the Republican party was the only way of saving these lands for free labor would have been an empty slogan to farmers and nonagricultural workers who were suffering from the effects of a severe and extended depression. Moreover, the failure of the North to act against the slaveholders who remained within the Union would have undermined its credibility with democratic forces abroad. Such developments would probably have delivered both a lasting blow to antislavery politics and an enormous fillip to nativist politics.

I do not maintain that the preceding sketch of what might have happened in the absence of a civil war is the only plausible one. However, it is a credible sketch of the likely train of events, one that is consistent with what we now know about the capacity of the slave economy of the South as well as with current knowledge of the political crosscurrents in the South, the North, and the rest of the world. At the very least, it points to reasons for doubting that there was a happy, relatively costless solution to the moral dilemma posed by Stampp.

I have not, it should be emphasized, put forward the gloomiest view of the alternative to the Civil War. The preceding sketch suggests an indefinite but more or less peaceful continuation of slavery. It would not be difficult to make a case for the proposition that peaceful secession would merely have postponed the Civil War and that the delay would have created circumstances far more favorable to a southern victory. In that case aristocratic proslavery forces would have gained unchallenged control of the richest and potentially the most powerful nation in the world. Such an outcome not only would have greatly increased the likelihood of rolling back the movement for working-class rights everywhere, but might have led to a loss of human lives far greater than the toll of the Civil War.

What the Civil War Achieved

As pacifists, [abolitionist William Lloyd]Garrison and his followers had to confront the dilemma posed by a violent confrontation
with the Confederacy. They reluctantly came to the conclusion that
bloody as it might be, the Civil War was the only realistic way of
ridding the world of slavery. William E. Channing, who had hoped
against hope that slavery could be ended by moral suasion alone,
explained why the destruction of slavery was the moral imperative
of his age. "Slavery must fall," he said, "because it stands in direct
hostility to all the grand movements, principles, and reforms of our
age, because it stands in the way of an advancing world."

What the Civil War achieved, then, was more than just inflated
wealth for northern capitalists and "half" freedom for blacks ("the
shoddy aristocracy of the North and the ragged children of the
South"). It preserved and reinforced conditions favorable to a
continued struggle for the democratic rights of the lower classes,
black and white alike, and for the improvement of their economic
condition, not only in America but everywhere else in the world.
The fall of slavery did not usher in the millennium, it produced
no heaven on earth, but it vitalized all the grand movements, principles, and reforms of Channing's age and of our own.

 **For Further Discussion**

Chapter 1
1. As part of his defense of slavery, John C. Calhoun asserts that slaves are treated well in the South. How else does he justify slavery? What evidence does Theodore Dwight Weld offer in opposition to Calhoun's argument?
2. What kinds of supporting evidence does Robert Liston use to support his assertions on the nature of slavery? What types of evidence does William K. Scarborough cite?
3. On the issue of paying black Americans for the harms of slavery, whose viewpoint do you find more convincing—Ronald Walters's or Karl Zinsmeister's—and why?

Chapter 2
1. How do the life experiences of Jupiter Hammon and Frederick Douglass differ? How might these differences account for their opposing opinions concerning slave revolution?
2. Larry Gara asserts that the legend of the Underground Railroad overshadows the role that runaway slaves themselves played in winning their freedom. Do you think this is true of Louis Filler's description of the Underground Railroad?
3. According to William F. Cheek, what motivated slaves to resist and rebel against their owners? What reasons does John B. Boles offer for slaves' nonresistance?

Chapter 3
1. Why does William Lloyd Garrison feel that gradual emancipation, as described by St. George Tucker, is flawed on both practical and moral grounds?
2. How different are the writing styles of abolitionists William Lloyd Garrison and Lydia Maria Child? What differing beliefs on how best to achieve abolition might underlie these dissimilarities in style?
3. Dwight Lowell Dumond criticizes William Lloyd Garrison for not contributing more substantially to the abolitionist move-

ment, but Russel B. Nye maintains that Garrison played an important symbolic role in the movement. Which appraisal do you find more convincing, and why?

Chapter 4

1. Are Abraham Lincoln's views on slavery, as revealed in the two viewpoints in this book, consistent with each other? Are they consistent with the Emancipation Proclamation, issued in 1863, which freed the slaves in the Confederacy but not in the Union?
2. Historians have debated the moral ramifications of the Civil War for decades. Based on the viewpoints by Jeffrey Rogers Hummel and Robert William Fogel and your own knowledge of American history, do you think the war's nearly 1 million casualties were justified?

 # Chronology

1619

The first black slaves to work on the North American mainland arrive at the Jamestown, Virginia, colony.

1641

Massachusetts becomes the first colony to mention slavery in its legal code.

1688

Friends (Quakers) in Germantown, Pennsylvania, draft the earliest antislavery document in America.

1700

Samuel Sewall writes *The Selling of Joseph*, the first antislavery tract published and distributed in the colonies.

1739

The Stono Rebellion takes place in South Carolina. The first major slave uprising, it begins when twenty slaves gather near the Stono River, south of Charleston. With stolen weapons, they kill local storekeepers and white families before being captured by the militia. Those blacks not killed on the spot are later executed.

1773

Slaves in Massachusetts petition the state legislature for their freedom.

1775

The first abolition society in America is organized by the Philadelphia Quakers.

1776

Thomas Jefferson pens the Declaration of Independence, with its reference to "all men" being created equal. During the 1850s Lincoln, among others, will make much reference to the fact that the word *white* was not inserted in this founding statement of American freedom.

1777

In its new constitution, Vermont becomes the first state of the now independent colonies to abolish slavery. Pennsylvania follows suit in 1780. Massachusetts courts rule that slavery is unconstitutional. Rhode Island and Connecticut provide for gradual emancipation beginning in 1784. New York and New Jersey make similar rulings in 1799 and 1804, respectively.

1778

Thomas Jefferson drafts the Northwest Ordinance, which bans slavery in the territory acquired from the British during the American Revolution. This is the first federal action against slavery and an important precedent for Lincoln and other "free soilers" (those who want no further expansion of slave territory) of the 1850s.

1787–1788

The U.S. Constitution is drafted and ratified. It includes three references to slavery, although the word *slavery* is never used: The slave trade is to be extended for twenty years; a fugitive slave provision is included; and the three-fifths compromise is devised, stating that a slave is to be counted as three-fifths of a person for purposes of representation and taxation.

1793

The federal Fugitive Slave Act is passed; it provides for the return of slaves who have escaped across state boundaries. A revolution of mulattoes and blacks in the French colony of Saint Domingue (Haiti) overthrows European rule there. Eli Whitney invents the cotton gin, producing an increased demand for slaves.

1794

The first national abolition society, the American Convention for the Promoting of the Abolition of Slavery, is founded.

1800

The Gabriel Prosser rebellion in Virginia begins and ends. Prosser, a blacksmith who placed himself in the tradition of the French and Haitian revolutions, planned to attack Richmond on August 30, 1800. Heavy rains delayed the plot, and whites learned of the plot from their slaves. The major conspirators, including Prosser, were eventually captured and hanged.

1807

Without significant opposition, Congress passes legislation that officially closes the slave trade as of January 1, 1808.

1817

The American Colonization Society is founded by members of the American elite, including James Madison. It seeks to return free blacks to Africa despite objections from free blacks themselves.

1819

Slavery returns to the national political stage when Missouri residents petition Congress for admission to the Union as a slave state.

1821

The Missouri Compromise is passed. It allows Congress to admit two new states, Missouri (slave) and Maine (free), to preserve the balance of slave and free states in the Senate. The legislation also deals with slavery west of Missouri by drawing a line (at 36° 30' north latitude) to the Pacific Ocean, north of which would be no slavery, and south of which slavery could exist.

1822

The Denmark Vesey conspiracy for the insurrection of thousands of free and enslaved blacks in South Carolina is foiled by black informers; Vesey and other conspirators are arrested and executed.

1829

Walker's Appeal, a militant pamphlet published by David Walker calling for slave rebellion, is distributed throughout the country, causing controversy in the South.

1831

William Lloyd Garrison breaks with the moderate abolitionists and publishes the first issue of the *Liberator*, which will be a major weapon against slavery for thirty-five years. Nat Turner's rebellion takes place in Virginia. On August 22, 1831, Turner, a preacher with a tendency toward mysticism, leads a group of black rebels in a series of raids that take the lives of some sixty whites, male and female, young and old. About two hundred blacks, including Turner, also lose their lives as a result of this revolt.

1833

The American Anti-Slavery Society is founded in Philadelphia by abolitionists, including William Lloyd Garrison, who favor an immediate and unconditional end to slavery. The state of South Carolina, with the open approval of the U.S. postmaster general, begins to intercept and destroy abolitionist literature sent into the state.

1836

Congress adopts the "gag rule," which automatically tables all abolitionist petitions, thereby preventing effective congressional debate on the issue.

1839

The most famous shipboard slave revolt occurs on the Spanish slave ship *Amistad*. John Quincy Adams argues on behalf of the African rebels before the U.S. Supreme Court; they are eventually freed.

1844

The Mexican War begins, raising anew the question of the expansion of slavery. Congress repeals the gag rule.

1845–1848

The annexation of Texas and the U.S. victory in the Mexican War spurs the debate on whether the newly acquired territories should permit slavery. The Wilmot Proviso is proposed, calling for no slavery in any territory acquired during the Mexican War. Although it passes in the House, it repeatedly fails in the Senate.

1850

The Compromise of 1850 is fashioned. California is admitted to the Union as a free state; a tougher Fugitive Slave Law is enacted; the slave trade is halted in the District of Columbia; and popular sovereignty is declared in the territories of New Mexico and Utah.

1852

Harriet Beecher Stowe publishes *Uncle Tom's Cabin*, which indicts not only slavery but also Northern complicity in it. The book is an immediate popular success in the North and causes great alarm in the South.

1854

The Kansas-Nebraska Act is passed, voiding the Missouri Compromise and possibly extending into territories north of 36° 30' latitude under the doctrine of popular sovereignty, a policy that gives the citizens of these territories the power to determine whether their territories will be slave or free.

1855–1859

Seven Northern states pass personal liberty laws designed to interfere with the Fugitive Slave Act by providing legal counsel to and requiring jury trials for alleged fugitives.

1857

The Dred Scott decision is handed down. The incendiary Supreme Court decision declares that blacks are not citizens and that neither the states nor the federal government can prevent the extension of slavery.

1858

The Lincoln-Douglas debates take place in Illinois, where Democrat Stephen Douglas's Senate seat is at stake. Also at stake is the issue of slavery expansion, as Lincoln argues for free soil and Douglas argues for popular sovereignty.

1859

White abolitionist John Brown's raid on Harpers Ferry takes place. Designed to lead to a general slave uprising, it ends in failure and Brown's execution.

1860

In November, Abraham Lincoln is elected U.S. president. In December, South Carolina begins the South's secession from the Union, which culminates in February 1861 with the establishment of the Confederacy.

1861

The Civil War begins. Congress passes the first Confiscation Act, which removes slaves from the owner's possession if those slaves are used for "insurrectionary purposes."

1862

President Lincoln proposes that states individually consider emancipation. He also asks Congress to promise financial aid to any state that enacts emancipation legislation. Congress passes the second Confiscation Act, which confiscates the property of those who support the Confederate rebellion, even if that support is limited to the paying of taxes to the Confederate government. Lincoln issues the Emancipation Proclamation, which formally frees the slaves in those states that have seceded from the Union but does not free slaves in the slave states that have remained loyal to the Union.

1864

Lincoln decides to lend his support to the idea of a constitutional amendment ending slavery. Such a proposal is included in the Republican Party platform for the 1864 presidential election.

1865

The Civil War ends. The Thirteenth Amendment, ending slavery, is ratified.

 # For Further Research

Historical Studies

Robert H. Abzug, *Passionate Liberator: The Life of Theodore D. Weld and the Dilemma of Reform*. New York: Oxford University Press, 1978.

Robert H. Abzug and Stephen E. Maizlish, eds., *New Perspectives on Race and Slavery in America: Essays in Honor of Kenneth M. Stampp*. Lexington: University of Kentucky Press, 1986.

Herbert Aptheker, *American Negro Slave Revolts*. New York: International, 1979.

John Blassingame, *The Slave Community*. New York: Oxford University Press, 1979.

David Brion Davis, *The Problem of Slavery in Western Culture*. New York: Oxford University Press, 1988.

Carl Degler, *The Other South*. New York: Harper and Row, 1974.

Martin Duberman, ed., *The Antislavery Vanguard: New Essays on the Abolitionists*. Princeton, NJ: Princeton University Press, 1965.

Dwight Lowell Dumond, *Antislavery: The Crusade for Freedom in America*. Ann Arbor: University of Michigan Press, 1961.

Stanley Elkins, *Slavery: A Problem of American Institutional Life*. Chicago: University of Chicago Press, 1976.

Donald F. Fehrenbach, *Prelude to Greatness: Lincoln in the 1850s*. Palo Alto, CA: Stanford University Press, 1962.

Robert William Fogel, *Without Consent or Contract: The Rise and Fall of American Slavery*. New York: Norton, 1989.

Robert William Fogel and Stanley L. Engerman, *Time on the Cross: The Economics of American Negro Slavery*. Boston: Little, Brown, 1974.

Eric Foner, *Free Soil, Free Labor, Free Men: The Ideology of the Republican Party Before the Civil War*. New York: Oxford University Press, 1970.

George B. Forgie, *Patricide in the House Divided: A Psychological Interpretation of Lincoln and His Age*. New York: Norton, 1981.

Elizabeth Fox-Genovese, *Within the Plantation: Black and White Women of the Old South*. Chapel Hill: University of North Carolina Press, 1988.

John Hope Franklin, *From Slavery to Freedom: A History of American Negroes*. New York: Knopf, 1947.

William Freehling, *The Road to Disunion*. New York: Oxford University Press, 1990.

Lawrence Friedman, *Gregarious Saints: Self and Community in American Abolitionism, 1830–1870*. New York: Cambridge University Press, 1982.

Eugene Genovese, *Roll, Jordan, Roll: The World the Slaves Made*. New York: Random House, 1979.

Herbert Gutman, *The Black Family in Slavery and Freedom, 1750–1925*. New York: Random House, 1977.

Michael Holt, *The Political Crisis of the 1850s*. New York: Wiley, 1978.

Winthrop Jordan, *White over Black: American Attitudes Toward the Negro, 1550–1812*. Baltimore: Penguin Books, 1969.

Aileen Kraditor, *Means and Ends in American Abolitionism*. New York: Ivan R. Dee, 1989.

Lawrence Levine, *Black Culture and Black Consciousness: Afro American Folk Thought from Slavery to Freedom*. New York: Oxford University Press, 1980.

Leon Litwack, *Been in the Storm So Long: The Aftermath of Slavery*. New York: Knopf, 1979.

John Lofton, *Insurrection in South Carolina: The Turbulent World of Denmark Vesey*. Yellow Springs, OH: Antioch, 1964.

Henry Mayer, *All on Fire: William Lloyd Garrison and the Abolition of Slavery*. New York: St. Martin's, 1998.

August Meler and Elliot Rudwick, *From Plantation to Ghetto: An Interpretive History of American Negroes*. New York: Hill and Wang, 1966.

Gerald Mullin, *Flight and Rebellion: Slave Resistance in Eighteenth-Century Virginia*. New York: Oxford University Press, 1982.

Russel B. Nye, *Fettered Freedom: Civil Liberties and the Slave Controversy, 1830–1860*. East Lansing: Michigan State University Press, 1964.

James Oakes, *The Ruling Race: A History of American Slaveholders*. New York: Knopf, 1982.

———, *Slavery and Freedom: An Interpretation of the Old South*. New York: Knopf, 1990.

Stephen B. Oates, *Fires of Jubilee: Nat Turner's Fierce Rebellion*. New York: Harper and Row, 1975.

———, *With Malice Toward None: The Life of Abraham Lincoln*. New York: New American Library, 1981.

Jane H. Pease and William H. Pease, *They Who Would Be Free: Blacks' Search for Freedom, 1830–1861*. New York: Atheneum, 1974.

Ulrich B. Phillips, *American Negro Slavery*. New York: D. Appleton, 1918.

Benjamin Quarles, *Black Abolitionists*. New York: Oxford University Press, 1969.

George P. Rawick, *From Sundown to Sunup: The Making of the Black Community*. Westport, CT: Greenwood, 1972.

Donald Robinson, *Slavery and the Structure of American Politics, 1765–1820*. New York: Harcourt, Brace, Jovanovich, 1971.

Willie Lee Rose, *Slavery and Freedom*. New York: Oxford University Press, 1982.

William K. Scarborough, *The Overseer: Plantation Management in the Old South*. Baton Rouge: Lousiana State University Press, 1966.

Richard Sewell, *Ballots for Freedom: Anti-Slavery Politics, 1837–1861*. New York: Oxford University Press, 1976.

Kenneth M. Stampp, *The Imperiled Union: Essays on the Background of the Civil War*. New York: Oxford University Press, 1980.

———, *The Peculiar Institution: Slavery in the Antebellum South*. New York: Vintage Books, 1956.

Robert Starobin, *Industrial Slavery in the Old South*. New York: Oxford University Press, 1970.

James B. Stewart, *Holy Warriors: The Abolitionists and American Slavery*. New York: Hill and Wang, 1976.

Sterling Stuckey, *Slave Culture*. New York: Oxford University Press, 1987.

Larry Tise, *Proslavery: A History of the Defense of Slavery in America, 1701–1840*. Athens: University of Georgia Press, 1987.

Richard Wade, *Slavery in the Cities: The South, 1820–1860*. New York: Oxford University Press, 1964.

C. Vann Woodward, *American Counterpoint: Slavery and Racism in the North-South Dialogue*. Boston: Little, Brown, 1971.

Jean Fagan Yellin and John C. Van Horn, eds., *The Abolitionist Sisterhood*. Ithaca, NY: Cornell University Press, 1994.

Document Collections and Other Important Primary Sources

John Spencer Bassett, ed., *The Southern Plantation Overseer as Revealed by His Letters*. Northampton, MA: Smith College, 1925.

John Blassingame, ed., *Slave Testimony: Two Centuries of Letters, Speeches, Interviews, and Biographies*. Baton Rouge: Louisiana State University Press, 1977.

B.A. Botkin, *Lay My Burden Down: A Folk History of Slavery*. Chicago: University of Chicago Press, 1945.

James Breeden, ed., *Advice Among Masters: The Ideal in Slave Management in the Old South*. Westport, CT: Greenwood, 1980.

William Wells Brown, *Narrative of William W. Brown, a Fugitive Slave*. New York: Johnston Reprint, 1970.

Richard Dorson, ed., *American Negro Folktales*. Greenwich, CT: Fawcett, 1967.

Rebecca Latimer Felton, *Country Life in Georgia in the Days of My Youth*. New York: Arno, 1980.

Philip Foner, ed., *The Voice of Black America*. New York: Simon and Schuster, 1972.

Jack P. Greene, ed., *The Diary of Colonel Landon Carter of Sabine Hall, 1752–1778*. Charlottesville: University Press of Virginia, 1965.

Frances Ann Kemble, *Journal of a Resident on a Georgia Plantation in 1838–1839*. New York: Harper and Brothers, 1863.

James McPherson, ed., *Blacks in America: Bibliographical Essays*. Garden City, NY: Doubleday, 1971.

Robert M. Myers, ed., *Children of Pride*. New Haven, CT: Yale University Press, 1984.

Willie Lee Rose, ed., *A Documentary History of Slavery in North America*. New York: Oxford University Press, 1976.

William K. Scarborough, ed., *The Diary of Edmund Ruffin*. Baton Rouge: Louisiana State University Press, 1972.

Robert Starobin, ed., *Denmark Vesey: The Slave Conspiracy of 1822*. Englewood Cliffs, NJ: Prentice-Hall, 1970.

Austin Steward, *Twenty-Two Years a Slave, and Forty Years a Freedman*. Reading, MA: Addison-Wesley, 1969.

Henry I. Tragle, ed., *The Southampton Slave Revolt of 1831: A Compilation of Source Material*. Amherst: University of Massachusetts Press, 1971.

Booker T. Washington, *Up from Slavery*. New York: Oxford University Press, 1985.

Norman Yetman, *Voices from Slavery*. New York: Holt, Rinehart, and Winston, 1970.

Websites

Born in Slavery: Slave Narratives from the Federal Writers' Project, 1936–1938, http://memory.loc.gov. This website contains more than twenty-three hundred first-person accounts of slavery and five hundred black-and-white photographs of former slaves. These narratives and photographs were collected in the 1930s as part of the Federal Writers' Project of the Works Progress Administration (WPA) and assembled and microfilmed in 1941 as the seventeen-volume *Slave Narratives: A Folk History of Slavery in the United States from Interviews with Former Slaves.*

Documenting the American South, http://docsouth.unc.edu. This website is a collection of sources on southern history, literature, and culture from the colonial period through the first decades of the twentieth century. It is organized into several projects according to subject, such as "First-Person Narratives of the American South," "North American Slave Narratives," and "The Church in the Southern Black Community."

Douglass Archives of American Public Address, http://douglassarchives.org. This website is an electronic archive of American oratory and related documents. The site is named after orator and former slave Frederick Douglass and contains several of his speeches as well as the speeches of other nineteenth-century leaders such as Abraham Lincoln, John C. Calhoun, William Lloyd Garrison, and Jefferson Davis.

 **Index**